MAGICAL SYMBOLS

of

Love & Romance

Richard Webster is the author of over 75 books and one of New Zealand's most prolific authors. His bestselling books include *Spirit Guides & Angel Guardians* and the new *Creative Visualization for Beginners*, and he is the author of *Soul Mates, Is Your Pet Psychic?, Practical Guide to Past-Life Memories, Astral Travel for Beginners, Miracles*, and the four-book series on archangels *Michael, Gabriel, Raphael*, and *Uriel*.

A noted psychic, Richard is a member of the National Guild of Hypnotherapists (USA), Association of Professional Hypnotherapists and Parapsychologists (UK), International Registry of Professional Hyponotherapits (Canada), and the Psychotherapy and Hypnotherapy Institute of New Zealand. When not touring, he resides in New Zealand with his wife and family.

Richard Webster

MAGICAL SYMBOLS

of

Love & Romance

Llewellyn Publications

Woodbury, Minnesota

First Edition
First Printing, 2006

Book design by Steffani Chambers
Cover design by Ellen Dahl
Cover images
　　Heart: © 2006 Digital Vision/Photographer Robin Cracknell/Getty Images
　　Background: © 2006 Artville
　　Tarot cards on cover from *Universal Tarot* by Roberto De Angelis;
　　　　used by permission of LoScarabeo.
Editing by Rhiannon Ross

Library of Congress Cataloging-in-Publication Data
Webster, Richard, 1946–
  Magical symbols of love and romance / by Richard Webster.
    p. cm.
  Includes bibliographical references and index.
  ISBN-13: 978-0-7387-1032-7
  ISBN-10: 0-7387-1032-6
  1. Symbolism (Psychology) 2. Love--Miscellanea. 3. Magic. I. Title.
  BF1623.S9W425 2007
  133.3'3--dc22

Llewellyn Publications
A Division of Llewellyn Worldwide, Ltd.
2143 Wooddale Drive, Dept. 0-7387-1032-6
Woodbury, MN 55125-2989, U.S.A.
www.llewellyn.com

Printed in the United States of America

Dedication

For my good friends in Seattle,
Sheila Lyon and Darryl Beckmann

Acknowledgments

I'd like to thank Princess Sofka, who introduced me to symbols almost forty years ago. I'd also like to thank Carl Herron (Brother Shadow) for his erudition and love of symbols. I'd especially like to thank him for his incredible enthusiasm for this subject. He has passed this enthusiasm on to many people, including me. His handmade symbols are the best I've ever come across. I'd also like to thank Rhiannon Ross, my editor on this project, for her hard work and dedication. Thanks also to the talented team at Llewellyn. It's always a joy to work with you.

Contents

INTRODUCTION

"Are not the charms of love of every kind,
and the enjoyment of beauty in all its forms in nature,
mysteries, miracles, or magical?"

Charles Godfrey Leland,
Aradia: The Gospel of the Witches

We are surrounded by symbols everywhere we go. Some of these, such as a cross or rosary beads, are obvious. However, others may not be recognized as symbols, at least at first glance. The American spirit is an example. This can be symbolized in many ways. The Statue of Liberty, the American flag, the Declaration of Independence, Pearl Harbor, and the Grand Canyon are good examples. Corporations spend large sums of money to promote symbols of their products. Wall Street symbolizes money and power to most people.

Most symbolism is universal, but there are exceptions. The dove is a symbol of peace for many people, but is loathed and despised by the Gypsies. This is because it is the only bird that kills for pleasure, rather than necessity. Consequently, for them, the dove symbolizes cruelty.

Magical symbols are images that conceal their true meaning. People who do not know what they are see them as images and pictures, but are not aware of the real meaning, which is hidden.

Most symbols are created from a combination of lines, squares, and circles, and each of these can have secret meanings. A vertical line, for instance, can symbolize the human spirit. It can also indicate the path from Heaven to Earth. A horizontal line symbolizes matter. It can also indicate movement from west to east, or from the past to the future. A square incorporates both horizontal and vertical lines, and symbolizes the material worlds we live in. The four sides also symbolize the four elements of Fire, Earth, Air, and Water. A circle symbolizes spirit, infinity, eternity, unity, Heaven, and the entire spiritual world. Someone who is unaware of this will look at a vertical line, for instance, and see only a straight line. Someone else, who knows the symbology, will obviously see much more.

The cross, created by two lines crossing each other at right angles, is possibly the oldest symbol in the world. It symbolizes prosperity and protection from evil forces. Christians associate the cross with the resurrection and eternal life.

There is a whole branch of symbology that deals with love and all its ramifications. Love is a common factor in every occult tradition, as it is believed that love is the essential unifying factor in the world. This is not only love between two people, but also the love that the creator has for everyone. This effectively unites the darkness of man with the light of God.

The powerful mystery of sex played an equally important role in ancient symbology. Not surprisingly, ancient people were fascinated with the continuity of life that they saw all around them, and created images of the male and female sex organs. At one time, people thought that these images revealed the bestial instincts of primitive people. Nowadays, they are considered to be a form of reverence towards the universal life force. The various depictions of the phallus, for instance, were intended to symbolize creative power. Consequently, there is no deliberate sexual element in many phallic shapes, such as church spires or maypoles.

Love spells and charms have been used throughout history to appease the gods and to help people find, and then keep, the right relationship. Care must be taken whenever magic is performed, as it is easy to accidentally perform black magic, rather than white. White magic can be performed to attract a partner. There is nothing wrong in doing this. However, it is black magic if you perform a ritual to persuade a specific person to fall in love with you. That might satisfy your needs, but takes no account of the needs and desires of the other person.

It is difficult to define love. Dictionaries describe it as a warm affection between two people. This may or may not include sexual passion or gratification. Unfortunately, this definition gives no indication of the many varieties of love.

Love possibly began when people realized how alone they were in the world, and started seeking emotional relationships for comfort and support. Ever since, love has covered the spectrum from enormous happiness to incredible heartbreak.

Because love is so hard to define, the ancient Greeks came up with several different words to describe various forms of love.

Epithemia describes the natural urge everyone has to touch and be touched or caressed. It relates to sensual love and the body's desire for sexual release. It could be considered a basic animal-like urge, as there were no romantic connotations associated with it.

Philia describes an idealistic idolization of someone else. It includes courtship, but excludes physical love.

Today, *Eros* means erotic love. However, it meant much more than this to the ancient Greeks. Eros was related to transformation, and the desire of two people to unite as one. Although transformation can provide sexual ecstasy, it can also produce pain and suffering. Eros also relates to mystery and the lure of the unknown. Consequently, eros can be hard to maintain in a permanent relationship, as the mystery soon disappears.

Agape is the love of god for man. Christians consider this to be an entirely sexless love, but in Greek times, gods frequently enjoyed sexual relations with mere mortals. Aphrodite, the Greek goddess of sexual love and beauty, is a good example. The word *aphrodisiac* is derived from her name. Two of her human lovers were Anchises, a Trojan shepherd, and Adonis, a youth of incredible beauty.

The Greeks may have had several words to describe love, but they didn't invent it. No one knows how or when love between two people began. An intriguing Paleolithic bone carving found in a cave in Isturitz, in southwestern France, may be the oldest existing depiction of love. It shows a man with his hands clasped, gazing up at a naked woman.[1] It is intriguing to think that this Stone Age picture may have been carved to attract love. Another contender for the oldest symbol of love is a small sculpture of a pregnant woman made from limestone. It is thought that this was an amulet carried by a hunter to remind him of his partner while he was away from home.[2]

Even if this carving was not a magical symbol of love, it did not take long to start. There is a four-thousand-year-old clay tablet in the University of Pennsylvania Museum that contains an incantation used by a priest to restore his client's lost love.

In the thirteenth century B.C.E., Hui, an official at the court of Pharaoh Ramses III, stole a book of magic spells from the Pharaoh's library, and used it to create wax figures intended to kill his master. He also made love amulets that he gave to the ladies in the palace, hoping these would encourage them to join his conspiracy. The plot failed, and Hui and his supporters were killed. This incident shows that amulets to attract love were being used at that time.

In India, the ancient Vedas contain numerous examples of love magic. The *Kama Sutra* includes information on how to use magic spells to attract a partner. The *Ananga-Ranga* was even more specific, offering to teach its readers all the magic they needed to know in order to attract, win, and enjoy a partner of the opposite sex.

---

1. Edward S. Gifford, *The Charms of Love* (London: Faber and Faber Limited, 1963), 2–3.

2. Denny Lee and Josh Stoneman, *Symbols of Love* (New York: Assouline Publishing, Inc., 2002), 8.

Magic spells to attract or enhance love are mentioned frequently in the writings of the ancient Greeks, such as Aristotle, Plato, and Euripedes. Retired prostitutes and witches from Thessaly and Phrygia found magic love charms a good source of income.

Magic was also popular in ancient Rome, but it was a dangerous pursuit as practitioners of the art faced the death penalty if arrested. Lucius Apuleius, a Roman satirist who lived about 200 C.E., married a wealthy widow. Her relatives, concerned that their inheritance was disappearing, took him to court claiming that he had used love magic to gain his wife's affections. His defense was that a young man did not need magic to captivate a forty-year-old woman who had been widowed for fourteen years. He won the case, and published his eloquent defense as *Apologia*.[3]

The Christian church condemned all magic, including love magic. Initially, the punishments were mild. Emperor Charlemagne (742–814) forbade any dealings with magicians or fortune-tellers. Offenders were placed in prison until they repented. However, in 829, Louis I (777–840), Charlemagne's son, better known as Louis the Pious, introduced the death penalty for anyone involved in magic. Many people were killed as a result, but this was nothing compared to the sixteenth and seventeenth centuries when thousands of witches were burned at the stake every year.

The celibate clergy had a prurient interest in love magic. They believed the Devil provided the necessary power for love

---

3. David Crystal, editor, *The Cambridge Biographical Dictionary* (Cambridge: Cambridge University Press, second edition 1994), 37.

magic to work. Nicholas Eymeric (c.1320–1399), the grand inquisitor at Aragon, wrote in his *Directorium Inquisitorium* (1376) that fortune telling, love amulets, and magic potions were all sacrilegious. This meant they were suitable targets for the inquisition.

In Britain, the penalties were not as severe. King Henry VIII passed an act in 1541 that said "it shall be a Felony to practice or cause to be practiced Conjuration, Enchantment, Witch-craft, or Sorcery, to get money or to consume any person in his body, members, or goods, or to provoke any person to un-lawful love." This was repealed just six years later. A new law, in 1563, sentenced people who "provoke any person to unlaw-ful love" to one year in prison, and time in the pillory every three months.

James I passed his famous "witch act" in 1604. This included death as the penalty for a second offense of "provoking unlaw-ful love." George II repealed this law in 1736, and replaced it with another that said practicing witchcraft was, in effect, fraudulent, as it did not exist.

Despite this change in the law, most people still accepted love magic, and stories about the successes and failures of love magic were invariably popular.

In 1591, Dr. John Fian, a Scottish schoolteacher, was forced to relate his experience with love magic while on trial for witchcraft. Apparently, he fell in love with a young woman in the village he lived in. When she spurned his advances, Dr. Fian asked her younger brother, one of his students, to help him. If he could obtain three pubic hairs from his sister, Dr. Fian would forgo the whippings that helped his students remember their lessons. The boy shared a bed with his older sister, and agreed to help. Unfortunately, his sister woke up when he tried to obtain the hairs, and the boy was forced to tell the family what he was doing. His mother cut three hairs from the family cow, and the boy gave these to the schoolmaster. Dr. Fian used the hairs while performing a spell to make the girl fall in love with him. The spell worked extremely well. The cow followed Dr. Fian everywhere, dancing and leaping around him while constantly mooing. The case attracted huge popular interest, and an engraving was sold that showed Dr. Fian drawing circles in sand while a cow gazed at him with love in her eyes. This humiliation was just the start of Dr. Fian's troubles. He was convicted of witchcraft, strangled, and burned at the stake.[4]

Another frequently told story concerns Archbishop Poppo of Trèves who fell passionately in love with a nun in 1030. The archbishop had given the nun a piece of his cloak to be made into special stockings for him to wear at Pontifical Mass. As soon as he put the stockings on, the archbishop felt incredible desire for the young nun. He soon suspected that the stockings had something to do with his unwelcome urges, and asked all the men in the cathedral to try on the stockings. Without exception, they all experienced the same feelings of lust for the nun. When the stockings were cut open, the archbishop discovered a magic charm. The nun was expelled from the convent and Archbishop Poppo went on a pilgrimage to the Holy Land to make amends for his sinful thoughts.[5]

---

4. Anonymous, *Newes from Scotland* (Edinburgh, 1591).
5. Edward S. Gifford, *The Charms of Love*, 41–42.

Naturally, there were many fictional stories involving love magic. Cupid's arrow is a good example of this. Cupid played a prominent role in Roman literature from about the time of Catullus (c.84–54 B.C.E.). Cupid is a winged boy who shoots arrows of passion that make his targets fall helplessly in love. Cupid symbolizes sensual love. Pathos symbolizes idealistic love.

Magical symbols of love and romance express their creator's feelings and emotions. Many people find it hard to express their feelings, and this frequently causes major problems in their relationships. People who can talk about their feelings while experiencing them are extremely fortunate. Other ways to express feelings are to keep a diary or journal, write poems, or create art or music. Negative emotions can be worked out of the system by going on a brisk walk or participating in some form of sporting or physical fitness activity.

Some symbols of love and romance are outside the scope of this book. Music is a good example. A friend of mine was falling in love when Phil Collins's recording of "A Groovy Kind of Love" was a big hit. This song became their symbol of love. Consequently, whenever they hear the song, they immediately relive the time when they first met. "A Groovy Kind of Love" is the perfect symbol of love and romance for them.

You will already know many of the symbols in this book, as they are part of our common heritage. Most people like to start working with symbols that they are familiar with. However, you will also find it fascinating to explore some of the symbols that you do not already know. If you find it hard to determine which symbol or symbols are right for you, trust your intuition.

The purpose of this book is to provide a wide selection of magical symbols that you can use to improve the quality of your love life. I have arranged these in different categories. Consequently, you do not need to read the chapters in any set order. In fact, you should start by reading the chapters that interest you most. Chapter fourteen provides suggestions on how to use the symbols to attain your goals. In addition, each chapter includes a case study of someone who has used a symbol to enhance his or her life. I hope you will enjoy reading this book, and will also find it useful as a reference book in the future.

CHAPTER ONE

The Sun, Moon, and Other Planets

When primitive man first tried to understand the mysteries of the world around him, he must have been amazed at the constant changes he observed when he looked up into the heavens. Stonehenge, and other stone circles, show that at the very least, primitive people were interested in following the sun's annual cycle. Sun and moon cults were followed in Babylon, Egypt, Palestine, Persia, India, Greece, Rome, and Gaul. The moon was worshipped long before the sun. In fact, in Babylonia, the sun was called "the son of the moon," not the father.

There has been much conjecture about this, but no one knows why there was so much emphasis on the moon. It may have been because the intense heat of the sun was harmful to crops. Consequently, the sun might have been viewed as an enemy, rather than a friend. Another possibility is that, unlike the moon, the sun was difficult to view. Also, the moon was always surrounded by a glittering panorama of stars and planets.

In most traditions, the sun symbolizes the male principle, and the moon the female. However, in some traditions, notably in Asia and some German-speaking countries, this is reversed because the inhabitants saw the sun as warm, nourishing, and maternal.

Cult of the Moon

The moon was the first Mother Goddess, which makes her the mother of all symbolism. Primitive people must have been fascinated with the different phases of the moon as it gradually grew from a thin crescent to a full moon, and then slowly diminished again. The four equal phases of the moon's cycle last seven days and gave people a convenient way to mark periods of time. Seven has always been considered a highly important, mystical number in numerology. The moon provided the first means of marking time, and the lunar calendar is still used in many parts of Asia.

Every month the moon imitated pregnancy, as it gradually grew larger and larger, before declining again. It did not take people long to make a connection between the twenty-eight-day cycle of the moon and women's menstrual cycles. As childbirth was vital to ensure mankind survived, people believed that the moon controlled the reproductive cycle. The moon became the "great mother." Gestation took ten twenty-eight-day lunar months, or forty weeks. This might also explain why the number forty has always been associated with difficulties or tribulations. God, for instance, caused heavy rain to fall for forty days and forty nights (Genesis 7:4). The wicked may be given forty lashes (Deuteronomy 25:3). Jesus spent forty days in the Wilderness (Luke 4:1–2). Lent, the period between Ash Wednesday and Easter, lasts forty days.

The light produced by the moon was believed to make plants and animals more fertile. Because moonbeams were believed to encourage pregnancy, women who desired to become pregnant slept under the light of the moon. Many witches removed their clothing to allow the light of the moon to reach every part of their bodies. This helped them reach their goal of fertility of mind and spirit, as well as body. People considered morning dew to be a magical liquid left by the moonlight. In fact, it was a common belief that a woman would conceive more easily after rolling naked in a meadow damp with morning dew.[6]

Another old tradition says that people can gain a dream vision of their future partners by speaking to the first new moon of the year. The following rhyme needs to be spoken while looking at the moon:

> *All hail to thee, dear moon, all hail to thee,*
> *I prithee kind moon, please reveal to me,*
> *Him/her who is my life partner to be.*

---

6. Raven Grimassi, *Encyclopedia of Wicca and Witchcraft* (St. Paul, MN: Llewellyn Publications, 2000), 147–148.

After this, the person is likely to see his or her future partner in a dream.

The Moon Goddess played an important role in early religion, especially in fertility cults. Elsewhere, she brought both life and death. The moon creates the tides in the ocean, and is also responsible for rain and floods. We need water to survive, but it can be a dangerous element for people caught in strong seas or bad weather. The moon has always been connected with fluids, and the menstrual cycle also reflects this.

The moon is also connected with strong emotions, such as love, and the inner world of intuition, which leads to premonitory dreams and psychic inspirations. The word *lunatic* comes from Luna, the Latin name for moon. Consequently, although the moon can encourage creativity and intuition, it can also cause insanity in some individuals.

The moon plays an important role in modern-day Wicca. Meetings are determined by the phases of the moon. Most covens meet when the moon is full, but some prefer to meet at the time of the new moon. The moon is at its most powerful when it is full, but the energy of the new moon is ideal for starting anything new. Any spells or magic that involve increase, healing, or gain are done while the moon is waxing (increasing in size). Magic for elimination or banishing is performed when the moon is waning. The three forms of the moon (waxing, full, and waning) personify the maiden, mother, and crone using the goddesses Diana, the Virgin Huntress (new and waxing), Selene, the Matron, (full moon), and Hecate, the Crone (waning).

The power of the moon is drawn down using an ancient ritual called "drawing down the moon." This ritual is so old that it is said Aphrodite taught it to her son, Jason. Aristophanes wrote about it in 423 B.C.E.

When you draw down the moon, you effectively draw her energy into every cell of your body. This makes it an extremely beneficial ritual to perform whenever you feel lacking in energy or enthusiasm. The best time to perform this ritual is outdoors on a clear night of the full moon. However, you can perform it any time by visualizing yourself outdoors at the time of the full moon.

Start by cleaning the area you are going to work in. If you are working indoors, you may want to vacuum or sweep the room before starting. If you are outdoors, you will want to choose a pleasant spot and bless the area you will be working in. You do this by gazing at the area and thinking pleasant, positive thoughts about it. Remove any rubbish or decaying matter.

Once you have done that, visualize a circle about six feet in diameter. You can mark the boundaries of this space, if necessary, by placing small objects in a circle around you. I have a circular rug of the right size that I use when working indoors. However, all that is necessary is to visualize yourself surrounded by a circle of protection.

Stand in the center of the circle with your feet apart. Take a few slow, deep breaths and then raise your arms above your head, with the elbows slightly bent. Visualize a pure white light descending from the moon and into your body. Stay in this position for at least sixty seconds, allowing the white light to reach every part of your body. You may feel the white light as a tingling or warming sensation as it spreads through you. You may feel strong emotions as the moon replenishes you. When you feel revitalized by the moon's (or goddess's) energy, give thanks. You can, if you wish, while still inside the circle, send healing thoughts to anyone who needs it. You may send healing thoughts out to the entire world.

You can perform this ritual as often as you wish.

Cult of the Sun

The power of the sun has been revered ever since primitive people settled into small communities and began planting crops. This marked the start of sun worship. The Egyptians and Babylonians changed from lunar time to solar time some five thousand years ago.[7] The ancient Egyptians were aware of the 365-day year, and added five intercalary days at the end of the 360-day zodiacal year to enable the system to work. These extra days were celebrated as the birthdays of Oriris, Isis, Horus, Typhon, and Nephthys, five important gods. In the seventh century B.C.E., the 365-day year was introduced to Greece.

In every part of the world where sun worship was practiced, the sun was seen as a handsome, young god who impregnated the earth with his warmth, vitality, and life. This, in turn, stimulated all living things to procreate and reproduce. The warm rays of the sun were also believed to bring good health, energy, peace, prosperity, and wisdom. It is not surprising that the cult of the sun god became so popular.

---

7. Ernest Busenbark, *Symbols, Sex, and the Stars in Popular Beliefs* (New York, NY: The Truth Seeker Company, Inc., 1949), 93.

There have been many love stories told about the sun god. Usually, they involve him directly, but there are also many that involve him in different roles. One of the most beautiful myths is the story of Scar-face, told by the Algonquian people of North America.

Scar-face was a young hunter who had received an ugly scar on his face after fighting a grizzly bear. Although this proved his courage and bravery, the other braves in the tribe endlessly taunted him about his looks. Like all the other braves, Scar-face was in love with the chief's beautiful daughter. After she discarded another admirer, Scar-face followed her to the river and proclaimed his love for her. The girl admitted that she loved him, too, but that she could never marry anyone as the sun god wanted her as his sun maiden.

"Is there nothing that can be done to change this?" Scar-face asked.

"Maybe you could find the sun god and ask him to release me from this promise," the girl said. "If he does, you must also ask him to remove the scar from your face. Then I'll know that he'll let me marry you."

Scar-face was despondent. He knew it would be almost impossible to persuade the sun god to give up such an attractive maiden. Nevertheless, he set out in search of the sun god. He crossed rivers and lakes, climbed high mountains, and battled his way through snow and ice. Everywhere he went, he asked the local animals if they knew where the sun god's lodge was. Eventually, he met a wolverine who said that he had been there a long time ago. He offered to take Scar-face at least part of the way.

After walking for many miles, they found themselves on the shores of a lake. The wolverine turned to go back, as he was unable to cross the lake without a boat. Scar-face was about to give up, too, but two white swans appeared. They carried him across the lake and told him which direction to take.

Scar-face walked for a long time. He found a bow and arrow, and paused to admire them. He left them where they were and kept on walking. Soon he met a young man who asked him if he'd seen his bow and arrow. Scar-face told him where they were and turned to carry on walking.

"Where are you going?" the boy asked.

Scar-face told him and the boy replied that he was Morning Star, the sun god's son. He offered to take him to meet his father. Morning Star's parents greeted him warmly and invited him to stay. Scar-face stayed for many moons, waiting for the right moment to ask the sun god for a favor. He spent his days hunting with Morning Star. Morning Star was allowed to go anywhere except near the lake, because of the fierce birds there that would kill him.

One morning, Morning Star disappeared as soon as they entered the forest. Scar-face knew instantly that Morning Star was going to hunt the fierce birds. He raced to the lake, arriving there just in time to save Morning Star from the birds. The sun god was so grateful to Scar-face for saving his son that he offered to do anything he could to help him. Scar-face explained why he had come to the sun god's lodge. The sun god listened in silence, and when Scar-face finished, nodded gravely.

"Go back to the woman you love and ask for her hand in marriage," the sun god said. "As a sign that I have granted this, I'll make your face whole again." He raised his hand, and instantly Scar-face's face was perfect. Before he left, the sun god gave Scar-face some magnificent clothes and ornaments to take back.

When he returned home, no one recognized him as he was wearing beautiful clothes and had a smooth face. The chief's daughter recognized him, though, and a few days later they married. Scar-face, now known as Smooth-face, and his bride built a beautiful medicine lodge to honor the sun god who had made their happiness possible.

Drawing Down the Sun

When you draw down the moon, you are summoning the energy of the goddess. You can call on the energy of the god by drawing down the sun. The process is identical. The only change is that you stand with your feet together, and cross your arms over your chest so that the tips of your fingers are touching your collarbones. Visualize yourself being filled with the sun's energy. As with drawing down the moon, this can be done by both men and women. There are times when we need female energy, no matter what sex we may be. There are other times when we require male energy. You can draw down the sun at any time you feel necessary. However, if possible, do not do this at the full moon, as this time is dedicated to the goddess.

Venus

Venus was the Roman goddess of love. Jupiter wanted her to marry Vulcan, but she thought he was ugly and unappealing. Instead, she took a variety of lovers, including Mars, who fathered her son, Cupid. Not surprisingly, as a result of all this, Venus is the planet most closely associated with love.

Venus is also associated with beauty. If you want to attract more love into your life, surround yourself with comfort and beauty. This is not necessarily an expensive exercise. You may add a few potted plants and a cushion or two. Playing beautiful music or burning scented candles are other ways to bring Venusian qualities into your home.

Venus's color is green. Anything green will add Venusian qualities to your environment. Consequently, an attractive potted plant will encourage growth and fertility in every area of your life, as long as you look after it.

Sandro Botticelli's famous painting, *The Birth of Venus* (c. 1485), was the first major Renaissance painting based on mythology. It depicts a nude Venus standing on a seashell floating on water. This is because Venus was born from the sea. To her left is a winged Zephyr, which is a personification of the West Wind. On her right is the Waiting Hour in the form of a beautifully dressed nymph. This painting is full of symbolism, and includes symbols of love. The nymph wears a girdle of roses and a garland of myrtle. Roses descend from heaven on the far left of the painting. These symbolize the pain of love. Venus is nude, which symbolizes love in all its various forms. This painting is the first to show a secular naked woman. Until the Renaissance, the Church considered nudity to be a sin and artists were not able to depict it.

Sun-Sign Compatibility

Many years ago, I wrote a book on sun-sign compatibility.[8] I was amazed at the amount of interest there was in the subject. Even people who expressed disbelief in astrology wanted to know what signs were the most compatible with theirs. Of course, sun-sign compatibility is only a tiny part of astrology. To determine your compatibility with someone else, you should ask an astrologer to draw up a compatibility chart for you.

However, almost everyone knows his or her sun-sign, making this a quick and easy way to assess the likelihood of a relationship.

The twelve horoscope signs can be divided into four groups using the ancient symbols of Fire, Earth, Air, and Water. These groups are known as Triplicities, because three signs belong to each element.

Fire: Aries, Leo, and Sagittarius

The Fire signs are enthusiastic, energetic, and active.

Earth: Taurus, Virgo, and Capricorn

The Earth signs are stable, patient, practical, and hard working.

Air: Gemini, Libra, and Aquarius

The Air signs are sociable and communicative. They enjoy mental stimulation.

---

8. Richard Webster, *Sun-Sign Success* (Auckland: Brookfield Press, 1982).

Water: Cancer, Scorpio, and Pisces

The Water signs are emotional, family-oriented, and naturally intuitive.

~

Looking at the elements provides some clues as to how the different signs will get on with each other. Libra is an Air sign. Sagittarius is Fire. Fire needs air to exist. Consequently, at a sun-sign level, these two get on. Look at Leo (fire) and Cancer (water). As water puts out fire, this is unlikely to be a good combination. However, there is no need to panic if you are a Cancerian married to a Leo. Your sun sign is a small part of your astrological chart. Any competent astrologer could erect a compatibility chart for you. A complete chart looks at all the possible combinations and permutations and will provide you with the full story. I am a Sagittarian and have been happily married to my Piscean wife for more than thirty years. Many years ago I read a book on sun-sign astrology that said we shouldn't even be in the same room as each other!

Symbolism of the Signs

Each horoscope sign has a symbol that provides a picture of the nature of the sign.

Aries (March 21–April 19)

The ram symbolizes Aries. A ram heads directly toward whatever it is he wants, and pays no attention to anything that might be in the way. The ram clearly illustrates the energy and immediacy of this sign.

Taurus (April 20–May 20)

The bull is the symbol of Taurus. At first glance, this may seem surprising, as Taurus loves beauty and culture. However, Taurus can also be extremely stubborn, and this is clearly shown by the bull. Taureans are also tenacious, persistent, and do not like to be pushed. They possess enormous latent energy. Again, the bull exemplifies these qualities.

Gemini (May 21–June 21)

The heavenly twins, Castor and Pollax, symbolize Gemini. People of this sign have good minds and enjoy communicating with others, usually vocally. They are changeable and adaptable, fitting into whatever situation they find themselves in. The duality, symbolized by the twins, enables Geminis to see both sides of a situation, which can create problems when they have to make up their minds. This duality also makes them changeable. They become interested in many activities, but lose interest in them quickly.

Cancer (June 22–July 22)

The word "cancer" means "crab" in Latin. Cancerians are soft-hearted, emotional people who often create a shell around themselves to provide protection from the onslaughts of a hard, uncaring world. Likewise, the crab has a hard outer shell that protects the soft interior. Cancerians love their homes, and sometimes use them as their symbolic outer shell. Crabs rarely head directly for what they want. They approach obliquely, and with many pauses along the way. Cancerians act in the same way. When dealing with Cancerians, it is usually better to appeal to their feelings, rather than logic.

Leo (July 23–August 22)

Not surprisingly, the lion symbolizes Leo. Lions are the king of the beasts. They are proud, regal, and "lion-hearted." Leos are exactly the same. They are natural leaders. They show off as they enjoy being the center of attention. Leos are positive, happy, pleasure-loving people. Although they can be thoughtless, they are generally sympathetic, generous, and kind.

Virgo (August 23–September 22)

The virgin symbolizes Virgo. This doesn't mean Virgos are destined to remain virgins. It shows that they are idealistic, virtuous, modest, dedicated, caring, and discriminating. Virgos are modest, unassuming, and gentle. They tend to avoid the spotlight, preferring to contribute in the background. They can be critical, aloof, and appear unresponsive.

Libra (September 23–October 22)

A balance, or pair of scales, symbolizes Libra. This is effective symbolism for people who always strive for poise, balance, and harmony. Librans are caring, sociable people. They prefer being married to spending life on their own. They appreciate beauty, and ensure that their homes are as attractive as possible.

Scorpio (October 23–November 21)

The scorpion symbolizes Scorpio. Scorpions have a sting in their tail, and this is frequently a trait of Scorpios, too. Scorpios never forget a slight, and repay any injury with interest. On the positive side, they never forget a favor or good deed, either. Scorpios are single-minded, emotional, intense, and rigid. Once they learn to harness these energies, their progress can be remarkable.

Sagittarius (November 22–December 21)

The Greek mythological centaur, half man and half horse, symbolizes Sagittarius. The centaur holds a bow and arrow. Sagittarians are like young centaurs. They are enthusiastic, cheerful, and energetic. The archer with his bow and arrow shows the "straight shooting" side of Sagittarius. However, they need to channel their energies, rather than shoot arrows in too many different directions. Because of this tendency, it often takes Sagittarians a long time to work out what they want to do in life.

Capricorn (December 22–January 19)

The symbol for Capricorn is the goat. This is a good choice, as people born under this sign are ambitious, cautious, determined, single-minded, and hard working. In the wild, goats climb mountains and reach the heights. Plodding, patient Capricorn subjects can do exactly the same. They have no time for flashy whiz kids, preferring to move ahead one step at a time.

Aquarius (January 20–February 18)

Aquarius is symbolized by a man pouring water. This surprises some people, as Aquarius is an Air sign. However, the water being poured symbolizes enlightenment, knowledge, and wisdom. The water-carrier is a well-known occult symbol that depicts the Aquarian Age. Before the Last Supper, Jesus told two of his disciples to go into the city "and there shall meet you a man bearing a pitcher of water" (Mark 14:13).

Aquarians enjoy learning and seek knowledge. They look for hidden truths and the reasons behind everything. Aquarians are natural humanitarians, but are also slightly detached, which can make it hard for people of other signs to understand them. Aquarians are unconventional, original non-conformists who enjoy making their own unique way through life.

Pisces (February 19–March 20)

The symbol for Pisces is two fish swimming in opposite directions. This clearly depicts the duality and indecision of the Pisces nature. However, it also shows that Pisces can swim with the tide, rather than fighting against it. Pisceans are naturally intuitive. They also possess strong imaginations and have a dreamy side to their nature. When they know what they want, Pisceans will work hard to achieve it. When they have no clear goals, they tend to drift with the tide.

Desmond's Experience

Desmond was a fifty-year-old accountant when he attended one of my psychic development classes many years ago. He was divorced and had been living on his own for ten years. Some years earlier, his daughter had given him a silver goat pendant for Christmas. This was because his sign was Capricorn. Desmond wore it around his neck, but underneath his shirt, as he didn't want his clients to see it.

At the time he came to my class, he had finally let go of all the baggage he had been carrying around since the break-up of his marriage, and was starting to think about seeking a new life partner. Despite the efforts of his friends and family, he had had no relationships since his marriage ended. When I asked him to think of something that symbolized love, he produced the pendant.

"Clarice, my daughter, gave this to me several years ago," he told us. "She loves me, so this goat symbolizes love for me."

One of the other class members pointed out that she had never seen it. Why did he wear it under his shirt? Desmond looked embarrassed.

"It doesn't look very professional," he said. "I'm an accountant, and I don't want people to think I'm superstitious."

This started a discussion. Some people agreed that it was better to keep it hidden, while others thought it should be in view. Finally, I suggested that he experiment with having it visible for one week. I could see doubt and fear in his eyes, but he agreed to try it.

A week later, at the next class, Desmond told us how he had fared. On the first day, a colleague had made a joking reference to the pendant, but the rest of his staff either made a favorable comment or ignored it. Desmond was more concerned about the attitude of his clients. He felt self-conscious at first when he noticed people looking at it, but the only comments he received were positive ones. After a few days, Desmond made the decision to keep the pendant in view.

When he met his daughter for lunch on the weekend, he found that she already knew what he was doing. His secretary had told her.

"I take it you're looking for a new woman," Clarice told him.

Desmond laughed at the memory as he told us about his conversation with his daughter.

"She seemed to know my intentions before I did." He fondled the pendant. "This is my lucky charm. I'm sure it will attract love to me."

It did not happen overnight. Desmond dated several women before finding the right one. By this time, the class had finished and I'd been wondering how Desmond was getting on. He phoned me one evening to tell me he was getting married again.

"Jane's one of my clients," he told me. "I've known her for almost twenty years. Nothing would have happened if she hadn't noticed my pendant. She immediately showed me her key chain, which had a bull on it. She's a Taurus. That started us talking about all sorts of different things. I invited her out for dinner, and everything went very fast after that. We're both very much in love, and very happy. Isn't it fascinating to think that if I'd kept my pendant under my shirt, none of this would have happened? My goat is a wonderful symbol of love."

CHAPTER TWO

The Human Body

The human body has always been used in symbolism. Man is considered the microcosm, compared with the macrocosm of the universe. This symbolism is not restricted to the entire body, either. The skeletal structure can be considered part of the Earth element. The skeleton, itself, is commonly used to symbolize death. The head, especially the brain, symbolizes Fire. The lungs, not surprisingly, symbolize Air, and blood symbolizes Water.

The Heart

The heart is one of the most popular symbols of love and happiness. The familiar heart symbol, which looks very little like the physical organ, is recognized virtually everywhere as a sign of love and passion. This association is extremely old. The primitive cave paintings of animals in France date back 26,000 years. A small red heart is painted in the center of many of them, showing that these people understood the heart's purpose and importance.[9]

Interestingly, the heart symbol is created from the number two and its mirror image. Two obviously means duality, or two people. The figure for two consists of a horizontal line and a curving vertical line, two shapes that are quite different from each other. This is similar to the Chinese yin and yang, the two opposites that cannot survive without the other.

The heart has had other symbolic meanings attached to it. It can represent the vital energy or soul that gives life. In Islam, the heart is considered to be spiritual and contemplative. In India, the heart is the part of the body where you contact Brahma. The Aztecs believed that the heart was, in effect, the body's sun. This led them to kill thousands of people every year to provide an offering of hearts to the sun. Obviously, this was the greatest gift they could offer.

The ancient Egyptians thought the heart was the home of the emotions and the intellect. The heart was left in dissected mummies so that it could be weighed in the underworld. The

---

9. Denny Lee and Josh Stoneman, *Symbols of Love* (New York, NY: Assouline Publishing, Inc., 2002), 14.

person's misdeeds in life weighed the heart down. The heart had to be lighter than a feather to continue on to paradise.

The ancient Greeks associated it with thought and feelings. However, this gradually changed and the heart became a spiritual symbol. In contrast to this, about three thousand years ago, the familiar heart sign symbol became related to the lyre, which was associated with Eros, the god of sexuality.[10]

In the Bible, we read: "As he thinketh in his heart, so is he" (Proverbs 23:7). This shows that, for thousands of years, people have believed that how we think in our hearts is much more important than how we think in our heads. There is an overemphasis on logical thinking today, but what the heart tells us will always be more important than cold, hard logic. The heart is the seat of love, sympathy, and compassion. It is interesting to note that the heart's electromagnetic field is five thousand times greater in strength than that of the brain. Sensitive devices called magnetometers can measure this energy from up to ten feet away.[11]

The heart is also a popular symbol in Christian art. The tradition probably began when St. Margaret Mary, a French nun, claimed that Jesus visited her and said: "behold this Heart, which hath so loved men that it has spared nothing." Although Pope Pius IX thought Sister Margaret was insane, he bowed to public pressure to have an annual feast in honor of Christ's

---

10.   Carl G. Liungman, *Dictionary of Symbols* (New York, NY: W. W. Norton and Company, Inc., 1991), 231.

11.   Doc Childre and Howard Martin, *The Heartmath Solution* (San Francisco, CA, HarperCollins, 1999), 99.

Sacred Heart. This feast is still celebrated today (on Friday of the third week after Pentecost).

A heart crowned with thorns was originally used to symbolize St. Ignatius Loyola (c.1491–1556), the founder of the Jesuits. A heart pierced with nails and crowned with thorns is a symbol of Christ's redeeming love. The flaming, pierced heart of Christ is a symbol of love for all mankind. A heart on fire symbolizes a devoted Christian, but Renaissance artists also used it to symbolize lust and profane passion. Its most likely original meaning was to show Christ's desire to be loved by humanity. The Renaissance artists also introduced the heart with Cupid's arrow embedded in it to symbolize love.

It is interesting that thousands of years ago, people chose the heart to symbolize love, as scientists have shown that the heart undergoes physiological changes when a person falls in love. This reaction can even cause pain in some people.

Blood

Blood is usually considered a symbol of the life force or the soul. Consequently, it is believed to contain divine energy. This energy was released during a human or animal sacrifice. In ancient times, people believed that an offering of blood caused rain and increased fertility. Consequently, in the Middle East, the bride stepped over sheep's blood that had been sprinkled in her path. Blood is also related to vitality and passion. Someone who is "red-blooded" is full of vital energy.

Blood has been mingled between two or more people to signify a union or sacred bond. One of the meanings of "blood brother" is a close friendship between two males that has been marked by commingling of blood.

Blood has special significance in the Christian religion. The wine that is drunk at Communion symbolizes the blood of Jesus.

However, in some traditions, blood is not considered in a positive light. Some primitive people think menstruating women are defiled and need to be segregated and cleansed.

Breasts

The breasts symbolize love, protection, fertility, and motherhood. However, a single bared breast can also symbolize humiliation and grief.

Hair

Hair normally symbolizes male strength and power. Samson lost his personal power when his hair was cut. Hair also symbolizes spirituality. When it is cut, it symbolizes the renouncement of earthly concerns. Both Buddhist and Christian monks shave at least part of their heads.

Hair also symbolizes sexuality. Groin and armpit hair appear at puberty. In some cultures, women's hair has a strong sexual element, which is why it is often covered. Part of the punishment for adultery was to have a priest uncover the woman's hair.[12]

---

12. Rowena and Rupert Shepherd, *1000 Symbols* (London, UK: Thames & Hudson Limited, 2002), 156.

Hand

Not surprisingly, the hand has always been considered a symbol of strength, authority, and power. It is a sign of openness and friendliness when a hand reaches out to another. This also has considerable legal implications, as when you shake hands to seal a contract or agreement, you are giving your solemn word. A handshake can also indicate a marriage agreement. The Hand of Atum was used as a fertility emblem in ancient Egypt.[13] The laying-on of hands to effect healing is an ancient belief, and shows that hands were believed to contain beneficial power. A blessing, given with the right hand, comes from the same belief. The left hand has always been regarded with suspicion, which is why blessings are bestowed by the right hand, and curses from the left.

Hindu and Buddhist mudras, or hand gestures, contain a wealth of symbolism. The hundreds of possible combinations are used in religious rituals, theater, and dance. The Anahata Mudra activates the heart chakra. To create the Anahata Mudra, hold your hands in front of you with all four fingers of each hand touching each other. Extend your thumbs and place the thumb of your right hand over that of the left. Create a gap between the second and third fingers of each hand, so that it looks as if you are creating two Vs with your fingers. This is the Anahata Mudra.

---

13. Atum, also known as Tem or Tum, was originally a deity of Heliopolis and was a manifestation of the sun god. Atum was thought to be the sun god's original form when he was in Nu, the primordial abyss. He is identified with the setting sun as it returns to the abyss, ready to be reborn in the morning as Re, the sun god during the daytime hours.

Handfasting

Handfasting is the name given to a marriage ceremony in the pagan tradition. Unlike Christian marriage ceremonies, handfasting is intended to last for the length of time that the love does, not until "death do us part." There is also a ceremony for divorce known as handparting. These ceremonies are legal if performed by a legally ordained minister. However, they are often performed either before or after a legal marriage ceremony. This is usually done to satisfy the entire family.

Mouth

The mouth has strong sexual symbolism. In Chinese symbology, it is sometimes associated with the vulva.

Kissing is usually a sign of love and affection. However, kissing can be done for other purposes. Judas betrayed Christ with a kiss. Roman Catholics kiss the ring of a bishop to express their loyalty. Muslims kiss the Ka'bah in Mecca as a sign of devotion. People kiss the hands or feet of kings, nobles, and judges as a sign of homage.

Navel

In West Africa, the navel is considered a symbol of fertility and motherhood. In addition to this, it also symbolizes the connection between mother and daughter, all the way back to the very first woman.

There is also a spiritual association with the navel. The temple at Delphi, for instance, was considered the world's navel. Mecca, the holy city of Islam, is considered by Muslims to be the navel of the world.

Phallus

In ancient times, the phallus was worshipped by fertility cults. It has always symbolized sexual power and fecundity. Konsei, the Japanese god of marriage, is phallic in shape. Ancient gods associated with fertility were often shown with an erect phallus. Priapus, the Roman god, and Freyr, the Norse god, are good examples.

However, the phallus was not always taken seriously. Satyrs were usually shown with huge erections that symbolized their libidinous, debauched nature. The Trickster, in the Native American tradition, is often shown with a phallus so large that he needs help to carry it around.

Uterus (Womb)

The uterus symbolizes Mother Earth. It is also a symbol of fecundity, fruitfulness, and abundance.

Vulva

The vulva usually symbolizes the mother goddesses and female procreative power. It also symbolizes the gateway to female mysteries and other hidden knowledge.

The mythical *vagina dentate*, or toothed vagina, symbolizes the fascination and fear that many men have of this organ.

Catherine's Experience

I have known Catherine for most of my life. She has never really been a friend, but our paths cross every now and again. She has a talent for establishing small business ventures, which she sells as soon as they are profitable. Some years ago, she attended a lecture I gave, and afterwards told me what she had done to attract a partner.

"After my divorce, the last thing I wanted was another relationship," she told me. "That lasted for about two years, and by that time, all my friends had given up trying to match me with suitable guys. When I felt ready, I bought myself two porcelain ornaments. One was of a really hunky guy. It was almost too much, but I thought if I was going to try to attract a guy, I wanted a real one! The other represented me, of course, and it was a demure, attractive maiden. The lady in the shop tried to get me to choose something that went more with the guy, but I thought this one was more me.

"Anyway, I got them home. I didn't want them where anyone could see them, so I put them in my bedroom, one at each end of my dressing table. After about a week, I pushed each of them about an inch closer to each other. I kept on doing this for a few months. Each time I saw them, which was several times a day, I'd think of what I was doing, and why I was doing it. It was my way of telling the universe that I was ready to start dating again.

"Every now and again I'd think it wasn't working, but then, just as I started to think I was wasting my time, a friend suggested we check out a new coffee shop in my neighborhood. I didn't go there hoping to meet someone. I just went for the coffee and to chat with my friend. Both of us noticed the barista. He was tall, good-looking, and looked as if he worked out a lot. The girl who took our orders was gorgeous, too, and I assumed they were a couple. Anyway, just as we finished our coffee, he came over and introduced himself. He was the owner, and he wanted our opinion on the coffee and the shop. We chatted with him for maybe five minutes and then left.

"The next day I was on my own and thought I'd have a coffee. I guess he was at the back of my mind, but I did really want a coffee. He was there again, of course. The place was quiet, so we chatted for maybe twenty minutes. At the end of it, he invited me out. I went straight home and put my ornaments in the center of my dressing table. They looked as if they were kissing.

"We had a good night, and arranged to meet again. All the same, things developed slowly. We were both involved with our businesses, and didn't have much spare time. It took about three months for us to become a couple, and we've been together now for almost five years. Do you think my porcelain figures helped me find Stephen?"

CHAPTER THREE

Marriage Symbols

he act of marriage is full of symbolism. It marks the essential union between male and female to create and nurture new life. The symbolism of wedding customs is shown in the wedding ring, joining of hands, and the presence of small children around the bride. The children are a form of sympathetic magic, and symbolize future children. The custom of throwing grain, rice, or confetti is another fertility symbol. Even the wedding cake can be seen as a fertility symbol as food is often used as a sexual symbol. The custom of breaking a glass or other small object at the

wedding reception has sexual overtones, too, as it symbolizes the consummation of the marriage.[14]

Wedding Cake

The tradition of a wedding cake goes back to Roman times when
a cake of meal was crumbled over the bride's head to provide
good luck. The wedding cake symbolizes good fortune and fertility. It also brings good luck to everyone who eats it. The wedding
cake should be made with an abundance of good quality ingredients to symbolize a long lasting, rich, and happy marriage.

The bride cuts the first slice of cake to provide good fortune in the marriage. Nowadays, her groom helps in this task,
to ensure that he shares the good fortune. This also shows they
will share all their worldly goods in the future.

There are a number of pleasant traditions surrounding the
wedding cake. One is that the bride puts aside a slice of cake
to ensure that her husband remains faithful. A tier of the cake
can be put aside for later use as a christening cake. This ensures
future children. Any unmarried women at the wedding should
take a piece of cake home with them and place it under their
pillows. This may produce dreams in which they see their own
future partners.

Wedding Gown

Bridal outfits are extremely important; none more so than the
wedding dress. Wedding dresses date back to ancient Egypt,
where the bride wore a dress of sheer silk that clung to her

---

14.   Jack Tresidder, *Dictionary of Symbols* (San Francisco, CA, Chronicle Books,
      1998), 131.

body and concealed nothing. Since then, more and more layers were gradually added, mainly for modesty reasons.

Queen Victoria broke with tradition by wearing a white wedding dress. Up until then, royal brides had always worn silver. Of course, after her wedding, every bride wanted to be married in white as it symbolized purity and innocence.

Nowadays, the bride is free to wear any color she chooses. It makes good sense for her to wear the color that is most becoming to her. An old rhyme from Warwickshire, England rather facetiously discusses different color possibilities:

> *Married in white, you have chosen all right,*
> *Married in green, ashamed to be seen,*
> *Married in grey, you'll go far away,*
> *Married in red, you'll wish yourself dead,*
> *Married in blue, your lover is true,*
> *Married in yellow, ashamed of your fellow,*
> *Married in black, you'll wish yourself back,*
> *Married in pink, of you he'll think,*
> *Married in brown, you'll live out of town.*

There are several variations of this rhyme.

As well as the dress, the bride had to wear "something old, something new, something borrowed, something blue." Because there is one more line to this verse (*And a silver six-pence in your shoe*) many brides place a coin in their left shoe to ensure the marriage will be prosperous.

"Something old" is ideally an object that belonged to a happily married old woman. Her husband had to be alive, as the magic did not work if she was widowed. This is an example of "sympathetic magic." The idea is that some of the good fortune that the old woman had experienced in her marriage would be passed on to the new bride.

"Something new" is usually the wedding gown itself. However, it can be anything at all.

"Something borrowed" originally meant something golden. Consequently, it was usually a precious piece of jewelry loaned by a relative. The gold object symbolized the sun, the source of all life, and wearing this borrowed object signified a union between the sun and the bride.

"Something blue" is to honor the moon, the protector of all women.

There are also a number of superstitions attached to the wedding gown. It used to be considered bad luck for the bride to make her own wedding dress. It was also considered to be tempting fate for the bride to try on the dress before her wedding day. Another superstition is that the bride should not look at herself in a mirror once she is completely dressed, before leaving for the church.

Bridal Veil

There are several suggestions as to the origin of the bridal veil. The most popular belief is that the traditional bridal veil was worn to conceal the bride's beauty from any evil spirits who might try to steal her away. Consequently, the veil could not be lifted until after the marriage had been solemnized. Another possibility is that the veil protected the bride from accidentally encountering the evil eye, which would be disastrous for the success of the marriage. The bridal veil may even have come from the East, where a man could not look at the bride's face until after she was married. Some folklorists suggest the veil signifies the bride's submission to her husband, but others say it indicates the opposite. The Greeks and Romans used a bridal canopy that was held over the bride and groom to keep the evil eye away. It is possible that the bridal veil is descended from that.

No matter what the origin, the bridal veil is still popular. Some brides like to wear the bridal veil of a friend or relative who is happily married. This is another example of sympathetic magic.

Bridal Bouquet

Flowers symbolize sex and fecundity. Consequently, the bridal bouquet symbolizes joyful lovemaking and fertility. The ribbons around the flowers are believed to bring good luck. There should also be knots, known as lover's knots, at the end of each ribbon. These symbolize unity and wholeness. Throwing the bouquet is a recent innovation. Whoever catches it will be the next bride.

Flower Buttonholes

A boutonniere, or buttonhole, is a flower or small bouquet worn in the buttonhole of a lapel. Boutonnieres were originally given to wedding guests to wish them luck.

Wedding Ring

The wedding ring is a perfect circle, with no beginning and no end. It symbolizes union, eternity, and completeness. No one knows where wedding rings originated. In ancient Egypt, married women wore grass bracelets around their wrists. This told other people that the woman was taken, and also signified that she accepted her husband's power and protection. The Romans introduced rings of precious metals, such as silver, gold, and platinum. As well as showing that the woman was married, it also showed the husband was prepared to trust her with valuable possessions.

The wedding ring has been worn on different fingers at various times. In ancient Greece, the index finger was normally used. In India, it was the thumb. The fourth finger was used for some time, until the third finger of the left hand became generally accepted. This dates back to an ancient Egyptian belief that a vein connected this finger directly with the heart. Once a ring was placed on this finger, the love was sealed in and could never escape.

During Victorian times, it was common for the bridesmaids to push a piece of the wedding cake through the wedding ring nine times. This meant she would meet her husband, and get married, within one year.

One of the most touching stories about wedding rings I have heard involves William of Orange (1650–1702). When he died, he was wearing on a ribbon tied around his neck, the wedding ring that he had presented to his wife, Princess Mary (1662–1694) in 1677. A lock of her hair was entwined around the ring.[15]

---

15. Megan Tresidder, *The Language of Love* (London, UK: Duncan Baird Publishers, 2004), 151.

Rice Throwing

Rice throwing is an ancient custom. It possibly began in the Orient where rice is a symbol of fertility, prosperity, and health. Consequently, throwing rice over the happy couple was an effective way to wish these qualities on the marriage.

The ancient Romans threw nuts and sweets of various kinds at the bride. The Anglo-Saxons tossed wheat and barley on the floor of the church for the bride to walk on.

Another possible source of this ancient custom is the belief that evil spirits were attracted to weddings. They were envious and jealous of the bride. However, they were also hungry and ate the rice, which kept them away from the bride.

Honeymoon

The word "honeymoon" comes from the ancient Teuton practice of drinking mead, a wine made from honey, for a month, or one moon's cycle, after the wedding. Apparently, Attila the Hun drank so much mead on his honeymoon that he suffocated and died.[16]

The honeymoon itself goes back to the time when a groom captured his bride by force and had to keep well away until the bride's relatives had ceased looking for her. It was a diplomatic move on the new husband's part to bring gifts for his in-laws when he brought his wife home.

---

16   Carole Porter, *Knock on Wood and Other Superstitions* (New York, NY, Sammis Books, 1983), 103.

Carrying the Bride Across the Threshold

The origins of this practice are no longer known. However, it is possibly related to the old practice of marriage by capture. Another possibility is that by carrying the bride over the threshold, she cannot stumble, as stumbling is considered a bad omen.[17]

Horseshoe

A horseshoe is considered a protective amulet against the evil eye. This probably derives from the fact that the horseshoe protects the horse. However, the crescent shape of a horseshoe reminded people of the moon and this encouraged other symbolism. Horseshoes can be hung with their prongs pointing either up or down. Masculine energy is produced if the prongs point upward, and female energy if they point down. Either way provides good luck.

There is a tradition of presenting a horseshoe, either real or decorative, to newly married couples. This gift is to wish them luck and to protect their home. The legend behind this concerns a blacksmith who later became Archbishop of Canterbury. St. Dunstan was working one day when a cloaked figure arrived and asked the smith if he would reshoe him, rather than his horse. St. Dunstan knew Satan had cloven heels that needed shoes. Obviously, his strange visitor had to be Satan. He tortured Satan with a red-hot poker until he agreed never to enter a house that displayed a horseshoe.[18]

---

17. Donald E. Dossey, *Holiday Folklore, Phobias and Fun* (Los Angeles, CA: Outcomes Unlimited Press, Inc., 1992), 193.

18. Peter Bently, *The Book of Love Symbols* (San Francisco, CA: Chronicle Books, 1995), 37.

Clarice's Experience

Clarice is my cousin's best friend. They went to school together, and both later became nurses. Clarice wanted to marry and settle down, but that was unimportant to my cousin, Fiona. As often happens in these cases, Fiona found her life partner well before Clarice. Before the wedding, Fiona used to joke that she'd throw her wedding bouquet to Clarice. Clarice was appalled.

"Don't do that," she said. "People will think I'm desperate."

At the wedding, when it was time to throw the bouquet, Fiona wanted to toss the bouquet to Clarice, but in her excitement couldn't see her. She threw the bouquet high in the air. As it came down, one of the young men at the reception flipped it up into the air again, and it landed in Clarice's hands.

"That was a definite omen," Clarice told me. "The bouquet wasn't thrown in my direction, yet it ended up in my hands."

Clarice took the bouquet home. For several months, she held it every day while thinking of her desire to meet the right man. In feng shui, dead flowers are considered negative. However, this did not apply in Clarice's case, as the bouquet was her symbol of love and romance. Each time she held it, she was reminded of Fiona's wedding, and the love the newly married couple shared.

Clarice met Tom at the wedding of another friend. She considers that appropriate, as she had been looking after Fiona's bouquet for several months. Clarice did not catch the bouquet at the second wedding, but she did not need to. By the time it was tossed, she and Tom were falling in love.

"I've never believed in love at first sight," she told me. "But it happens. It was as if Tom and I had known each other forever. I kept asking myself if it was the fact that we were at a wedding, or maybe the alcohol, but it was neither. We met and fell in love, all within minutes."

Clarice still has Fiona's wedding bouquet, as it will always be her symbol of love and romance.

CHAPTER FOUR

Animal Symbols

nimals have always been used to symbolize different energies, as well as our own animal emotions.
Bears usually symbolize grumpiness, for instance. A bull
symbolizes stubbornness, while a dog represents loyalty. An
elephant symbolizes good memory. A fox makes us think of
cunning. A lion symbolizes courage, while a mouse symbolizes timidity. These associations are universal, and came
about as a result of observation.

Animals have been used symbolically since cave man days.
Rock paintings inside caves frequently depict animals. Painting

an animal surrounded by hunters on the wall of a cave may well have been a form of sympathetic magic.

In religion, many gods were represented by animals or animal heads. Ganesh, the Hindu god of wisdom, is a good example. He has the head of an elephant. In Christianity, the dove is used as a symbol of the Holy Spirit.

Throughout history, animals have been used to symbolize human traits. Wise as an owl, cunning as a fox, and faithful as a dog are all examples of this. Mythical animals, such as the dragon, sphinx, and unicorn, are also rich in symbolism. Mythology is full of hybrid animals that are half human and half beast. The centaur of Greek mythology has the head of a man and the body of a horse. The centaur is associated with lust, drunkenness, and violence, and symbolized the animalistic side of humankind. Mermaids appear regularly in sailing folklore. A strange creature, consisting of a human body and an animal's head, is depicted on The Wheel of Fortune card in the Tarot deck. This animal could be an indication that mankind is still evolving. Although the body is recognizably human, the head has not yet developed into human form.[19] When I first learned the Tarot, I was taught that this animal is Anubis, the Egyptian god of tombs and embalming who weighed the hearts of the dead. He had the body of a man and the head of a jackal. The snake on the left side of the wheel is Set, brother of Osiris and the Egyptian god of death. Consequently, Set symbolizes death, and Anubis symbolizes rebirth.

---

19. Naomi Ozaniec, *Initiation into the Tarot* (London, UK: Watkins Publishing, 2002), 34.

The unicorn symbolizes virginal purity. This is because its single horn, a phallic symbol, is attached to the forehead, home of the mind, which sublimates the sexual potential into potentially more worthwhile areas. Mary, mother of Jesus, is frequently pictured with a unicorn in her lap. This symbolizes the Immaculate Conception. Other animals that symbolize chastity are the bee, dove, elephant, phoenix, and salamander.

Naturally, there are also animals that symbolize lust. These include the ape, ass, bear, cat, cock, goat, horse, leopard, monkey, pig, and rabbit. In Christian art, snakes or toads feeding on the breasts of women are sometimes used to symbolize lust.

Bee

The bee symbolizes industry, prosperity, sweetness, and diligence. The bee also symbolizes virginity, chastity, and purity. This association came about because people used to believe the bee reproduced asexually. In ancient Egypt, the bee was known as the "giver of life" and symbolized birth, death, and reincarnation. It also symbolized a successful, happy, productive, fruitful life. In ancient Greece, Demeter was known as the queen of the bees. Bees were associated with Cupid who used them to sting people who fell in love.

Bull

The bull is a powerful symbol of male potency. In the past, a family's wealth was determined by the number of cattle they possessed. Bulls, in particular, became associated with wealth, power, and sexual prowess. A bull market indicates a powerful, surging stock market. (See also Cow.)

Butterfly

In Japan, the butterfly symbolizes femininity. Two butterflies symbolize a happy marriage. Around the world, the butterfly symbolizes the soul, which cannot be extinguished as the butterfly develops from the egg, into a caterpillar, chrysalis, and ultimately, butterfly.

Cat

Cats were sacred animals in ancient Egypt. Bastet was a feline-headed, lunar goddess who was associated with pleasure, fertility, and protection. Over the centuries, cats have had a mixed reputation. Buddhists, for instance, believe that cats failed to mourn the death of Buddha. The association of cats with demonic forces was a common belief in Europe in the Middle Ages.

An unexpected appearance of a cat indicates sexual issues that need to be examined and healed.

Cow

The cow is a maternal symbol. Both the cow and the bull are also considered fertility symbols. Early civilizations considered the cow to symbolize Mother Earth. Some people took this further, relating the cow's curved horns to the moon, and her milk with the Milky Way. Nut, the Egyptian goddess of the sky, was sometimes represented as a cow with stars on her stomach, and her four legs indicated the four quarters of the earth. The cow is a sacred animal in India. In Vedic literature, the cow symbolizes both the earth and sky, and her milk symbolizes live-preserving, fertilizing rain.

Deer

The stag, a male deer, symbolizes passion, ardor, and virility. When deer were introduced into Australia, they quickly became important symbolic animals to the Aborigines. They believe that to dream of a deer is a sign of unconditional love and of living in harmony with all living things.[20]

Dog

The usual symbolism of a dog is as "man's best friend." This means that it serves as a masculine symbol of loyalty, love, steadfastness, and protection.

Dove

The dove symbolizes love, purity, peace, and hope. Today the dove is a peace symbol. This is due largely to the favorable references the dove received in the Bible. A dove returned to Noah with an olive branch as a sign of peace. After he baptized Jesus, John the Baptist "saw the Spirit descending from heaven like a dove" (John 1:32).

Christians also associated the dove with chastity, in marked contrast to earlier symbolism. Depictions of winged phalluses and doves were found together in the ruins of Pompeii. The moaning sound produced by the dove reminded people of both sex and childbirth.

An old folk custom says that you can ensure your love will continue to love you forever if you conceal the dried tongue of

---

20. Scott Alexander King, *Animal Dreaming* (Warburton, Australia: Circle of Stones, 2003), 60.

a turtledove in his or her bedroom. A pair of doves symbolizes a long, harmonious marriage.

Duck

In Asia, ducks, especially the Mandarin duck, symbolize a happy marriage, constancy, and fidelity. Pairs of ducks are common emblems of marriage, and can be found as decorations in honeymoon suites in both Japan and China.

Eagle

The eagle has always been considered a powerful, even regal, symbol. The ancient Greeks considered this bird a spiritual symbol, which is why an eagle attends Zeus. In Sumerian and Assyrian mythology, the eagle symbolized fertility.

Elephant

The elephant symbolizes power, royalty, patience, wisdom, and retentive memory. It also symbolizes a strong sex drive and a successful and passionate marriage.

Fish

The fish has always been considered a symbol of fertility and sexual happiness. There are three main reasons for this. Plutarch wrote that the ancient Egyptians considered fish to be phallic symbols.[21] Fish produce copious amounts of spawn. Water, itself, is also a fertility symbol. In China, two fish symbolize marriage and fruitfulness. The Celts tell a story about Tuan MacCairill who had several incarnations. In one of them,

---

21.   Elisabeth Goldsmith, *Ancient Pagan Symbols* (New York: G. P. Putnam's Sons, Inc., 1929), 122.

he was a salmon. In this incarnation, he impregnated an Irish queen who ate him after he was caught.[22]

Frog

The frog is an amphibious animal. As it comes from the water, it is considered a symbol of transformation, rebirth, and renewal. It is also a symbol of earthly pleasures. As such it is associated with eroticism, lust, and fertility.

Goat

Goats have always symbolized lust and virility. Female goats are also associated with fecundity and nourishment. A female goat nursed the Greek god Zeus. A number of fertility cults, including the Mendesians of Egypt, used goats in a variety of ways. Herodotus wrote that the Mendesians practiced bestiality.

Goose

The Celts and Chinese considered the goose a masculine symbol. The term "goosing" relates to the sexual symbolism of the goose, which dates back to Priapus in ancient Greece. In much of central Asia, "goose" is an affectionate term used by men when referring to their wives.[23] In China, the goose is called the "Bird of Heaven" and symbolizes love, faithfulness, truth, and inspiration.

---

22. Edain McCoy, *Celtic Myth and Magick* (St. Paul, MN: Llewellyn Publications, 1995), 343.
23. Udo Becker (translated by Lance W. Garmer), *The Continuum Encyclopedia of Symbols* (New York, NY: Continuum Publishing Company, 1994), 130. (Originally published 1992 by Verlag Herder Freiburg im Breisgau.)

Hippopotamus

In ancient Egypt, the hippopotamus was considered the embodiment of brutality and evil. This came about because of its methods of capturing and eating its prey. It may seem surprising that the hippopotamus was also considered a protector of women, and symbolized pregnancy. Statues of upright, pregnant hippopotami goddesses were commonly found in people's homes to encourage pregnancy.

Horse

The horse has always been a benevolent symbol of strength, endurance, stamina, intelligence, and devotion. The horse is also a masculine symbol of sexual passion and potency.

Kangaroo

The kangaroo carries its young in a pouch. Consequently, it symbolizes domestic harmony and a stable home and family life.

Kingfisher

In China, the graceful, regal kingfisher is a symbol of domestic harmony and a happy marriage. This probably came about because they often fly in pairs. The kingfisher also symbolizes clear vision, tranquillity, and peace of mind.

Magpie

In China, the magpie symbolizes sexual compatibility and a successful marriage. This probably derives from the ancient Chinese custom of breaking a mirror in half when a husband and wife are forced to be apart for any length of time. Each partner keeps one half. The belief is if either partner is unfaithful, their half of the mirror will turn into a magpie and fly to the other partner to tell them what happened.[24]

Nightingale

Because it has such a sweet, yet sad-sounding song, the nightingale symbolizes the agony and ecstasy of love. In Greek legend, Philomela had her tongue cut out to prevent her from telling people that her brother-in-law, Tereus, had raped her. Consequently, the nightingale also symbolizes pain and suffering.

Otter

The otter symbolizes sexual activity. In fact, the male otter's sex drive is so strong, a Chinese folk belief says that a male otter will make love to a tree if it cannot find a female partner. Consequently, a powder made from an otter's penis is considered an effective aphrodisiac.

Ox

Most of the symbology concerning the ox represents strength, force, and protection. It symbolizes masculine energy, reproduction, and fertility.

Oyster

The oyster symbolizes female sexuality and fertility. This is because it lives in water (fertility) and its shape resembles the vulva.

---

24. Wolfram Eberhard (translated by G. L. Campbell), *A Dictionary of Chinese Symbols* (London, UK: Routledge & Kegan Paul, Limited, 1986), 174. (Originally published in German as *Lexicon chinesischer Symbole* by Eugen Diederichs Verlag, 1983.)

Partridge

The partridge symbolizes feminine beauty, love, and fruitfulness. It was associated with Aphrodite, the Greek goddess of love. A folk tradition claimed its flesh was an aphrodisiac.

Pelican

The pelican symbolizes the love parents have for their children. An ancient Greek story told how the pelican killed its ugly children, and then brought them back to life three days later using blood from self-inflicted wounds.

Pig

Pigs are symbolized in a variety of ways. They are an emblem of gluttony, selfishness, and stubbornness. However, they also symbolize fertility, fecundity, motherhood, and happiness. The pig is also considered to symbolize fertility and virility in China.

Rabbit

The rabbit is associated with the moon, procreation, fertility, and lust. Because they are such prolific breeders, rabbits have been used in attempts to cure impotence and sterility using sympathetic magic. The Easter Bunny hands out eggs, another popular fertility symbol.

Ram

The ram symbolizes Aries, the first sign of the Zodiac. As such, it represents fertility, spring, and new growth. The ram symbolizes lust and virility. The ram's horns serve as phallic symbols.

Rooster

The rooster symbolizes male sexuality and fertility. This symbolism has gradually become distorted, and today the proud, strutting rooster represents overly macho-type behavior.

Snake

The snake is arguably the oldest animal symbol. Prehistoric rock paintings frequently include snakes, possibly as a fertility symbol. Snakes remind people of both the penis and the umbilical cord, which provides a wealth of sexual symbolism. It was a snake that tempted Eve to take the forbidden fruit in the Garden of Eden. As a result of this, the snake has been considered a symbol of sexual passion.

Sparrow

In China, the flesh of the sparrow is believed to possess aphrodisiacal qualities. The sparrow symbolizes the penis. Similar associations have also occurred in the West. The sparrow was associated with the goddess Aphrodite in ancient Greece. In Western art, a woman holding a sparrow signifies someone who is lewd and lascivious.

Squirrel

The squirrel is considered a fertility symbol in Japan. It hasn't fared so well in the West, where, apart from children's picture books, it is usually considered a destructive rodent. In the Middle Ages, it was a symbol of the devil because of its bright red color and incredible speed.

Stork

Many children in the West are told that a stork delivers babies. This fable comes from ancient Greece where the stork was sacred to Hera, goddess of marriage, women, and childbirth. As the stork was believed to be a good parent, it gradually became connected with Hera, and the myth began. The stork was also believed to look after its aging parents.

Swallow

The arrival of the swallow marks the start of spring. Because of this association with rebirth and new life, the swallow symbolizes childbirth. It is also associated with domesticity and a happy home and family life.

Swan

The swan symbolizes beauty, love, passion, and the gradual decay of these. Wagner's opera *Lohengrin* tells the story of a swan knight. Tchaikovsky's ballet *Swan Lake* focuses on the beauty and perceived femininity of the swan. In Greek myth, Zeus disguised himself as a swan to seduce Leda.

Tortoise

The tortoise is revered in China because the markings on a tortoise shell inspired the I Ching, feng shui, and Chinese numerology.[25] People believed the tortoise could conceive using nothing but the power of thought. It was considered a symbol of longevity, patience, and fecundity. In China, the tortoise is considered a female symbol, but in parts of Africa, it has been

---

25. Richard Webster, *Feng Shui for Beginners* (St. Paul, MN: Llewellyn Publications, 1997), 1.

associated with the male. This is because the emerging head and neck are considered penile.

Unicorn

The unicorn is a mythological animal that has been an important symbol for at least two thousand years. In the fifth century B.C.E., Ctesias, a Greek historian and physician, mentioned the healing powers of the unicorn's horn in *Persica*, his history of Persia and Assyria.[26]

Early Christians considered the unicorn to be an emblem of female chastity. This was because of an old legend that said unicorns could only be caught by virgins who were pure in body and mind.

There is an obvious phallic association with the unicorn's horn. This became a symbol of spiritual penetration that explained the appearance of Jesus in the Virgin's womb.[27] However, the horn's placement on the forehead also shows the power the mind has to sublimate lust.

Cassandra's Experience

Cassandra, a student of mine, was experiencing marital problems. After ten years of marriage, she and her husband were drifting apart. Neither was involved with anyone else, but the closeness and fun had disappeared. They made love less and less frequently, and Cassandra could not remember when they had last cuddled each other on the couch.

---

26. David Crystal (editor), T*he Cambridge Biographical Encyclopedia* (Cambridge, UK: Cambridge University Press, 1998), 243.

27. Jack Tresidder, *Dictionary of Symbols*, 214.

Shortly after we had discussed animal symbolism, Cassandra's mother died. Cassandra's mother had had a large collection of cat ornaments, and she and her two brothers split the collection into thirds. She took her cats home and displayed them in the living room.

"I wasn't thinking about animal symbolism at the time," she told me. "I thought I was creating a sort of memorial to my mother."

However, once she had done this, Cassandra began to notice small, almost imperceptible improvements in her marriage. One night her husband put his arm around her as they watched television. This was something he had not done for months. He started making favorable comments on how good she looked, and their lovemaking became more frequent and fulfilling.

Cassandra told us that although her husband had never mentioned her collection of cats, she sometimes saw him looking at them. Occasionally, he'd pick up one of the ornaments, and examine it closely before replacing it. It was this that made her realize what was going on.

"Quite unwittingly, these cats became my symbols of love," she told us. "I still haven't discussed that with Brent, as I think he'd laugh at the idea. But he'd have to admit our relationship is better now than it ever has been."

*P*lants, in every form, have always contained strong symbolism. Their annual cycle symbolizes death (winter) and resurrection (spring). More importantly, for the purposes of this book, the profusion and abundance of vegetation symbolizes fertility and fecundity. Even today, many celebrations are conducted to thank the cosmic forces for allowing the annual rebirth to continue. The Wiccan sabbat of Beltane on May 1st is an example. This marks the annual courtship of the God and Goddess. Beltane was originally a Celtic celebration of new life and fertility.

The vegetable kingdom is the source of many symbols of love and romance. Some of these are obvious, because of their appearance. Carrots and bananas are good examples of this. Peas may seem less obvious, yet they used to be tossed into the laps of young brides to ensure fertility. Peas and beans are good symbols of fertility and fruitfulness. Bean fields were popular places for courting. This is because it was believed that the mere scent of beans aroused the passions of women.

Herbs and other plants were common ingredients in medieval love spells. Magicians would prepare a paste containing foxglove and nightshade. If this was applied to the eyelids of a sleeping man, he would propose marriage as soon as he awoke.

Aphrodisiacs come in a variety of shapes and forms. Garlic was considered especially good because it cleansed the blood and gave strength and stamina. Asparagus is also reputed to possess strong aphrodisiacal qualities. Nicholas Culpeper (1616–1654) wrote that they "stirreth up bodily luste in men and women." The ancient Romans used to include lettuce in their banquets, as it was believed to encourage sexual performance. In Elizabethan times, tomatoes were nicknamed "love apples." The Aztecs believed avocados were aphrodisiacs.

Almond

The almond symbolizes virginity and potential fruitfulness. The legend of Attis says he was conceived from an almond. This is because ancient people equated the juice from pressed almonds with semen. They also related the shape of an almond to the vagina. This ultimately led to a European folk tradition that said that virgins could become pregnant if they slept under an almond tree and happened to dream of the person she loved.

The almond is also said to attract undying love. The ancient Greeks had a legend to explain this. Demephon, a soldier, was engaged to Phyllis, a beautiful princess. Unfortunately, Demephon arrived at the wedding several months late. In the meantime, Phyllis, feeling rejected, had hanged herself. The gods felt sorry for her and turned her into an almond tree. Demephon offered a sacrifice to the tree, which immediately blossomed, even though no other tree in the area had any flowers on it. Consequently, young lovers sometimes carry almonds as a lucky charm, confident that it will provide undying love.

Apple

Ever since the time of Adam and Eve, the apple has been the ultimate symbol of love, romance, and sexual desire. Eating the apple marked the end of their innocence. "And the eyes of them both were opened, and they knew that they were naked" (Genesis 3:7).

When an apple is sliced in half horizontally, rather than vertically, the core creates a perfect five-pointed star. This pentagram is related to Venus, the Roman goddess of love. This is why it is believed Eve gave Adam an apple, rather than some other fruit.

The Lovers card in the *Mythic Tarot* shows the mythic story of the Judgment of Paris. Paris holds a golden apple while determining the fairest of three goddesses: Hera, Athena, and Aphrodite.

The apple has been used in many ways to encourage love. If a young girl held a lighted candle in front of a mirror on Halloween while eating an apple, she would see the reflection of her future husband in the mirror. Another pastime was to peel an apple into one long strip and then toss it backwards over your left shoulder. If you were fortunate, the peel would form a letter of the alphabet, and this would be the first letter of your future husband's name. Yet another tradition says that you should pick an apple by twisting the stem. The first twist corresponds to the letter "A," the second "B," and so on, until the apple breaks off. The final letter you choose will be that of someone who loves you.

Barley

Barley grains symbolize fertility and new life. The ancient Greeks used barley sheaves to symbolize fruitfulness.

Basil

During Elizabethan times, bachelors often carried basil leaves in their pockets when seeking a partner. They believed this would create the right atmosphere for a sympathetic hearing. Basil leaves symbolized love, but were not supposed to be seen by others. Would-be suitors were ridiculed if they accidentally pulled the basil leaves from their pockets.

Caraway

The ancient Greeks prescribed caraway to young girls who were lacking in energy. In Tudor times, caraway seeds were considered useful as aphrodisiacs. King Henry VIII is reputed to have drunk a glass of mulled wine and caraway seeds before going to bed. In Shakespeare's *Henry IV, Part 2*, Sir John Falstaff says: ". . . you shall see my orchard, where, in an arbour, we will eat a last year's pippin of my own graffing with a dish of caraways, and so forth" (Act V, scene 3, lines 1–3). Today, caraway is an important ingredient in Kümmel liquor.

Cypress

The cypress is considered a phallic symbol. In this guise, it represents virility, stamina, and numerous descendants. The cypress is a symbol of loyalty, patience, and steadfastness in the Christian tradition. The cypress symbolized the gods in the Greek and Roman traditions.

Date (see also Palm Tree)

The date is an ancient symbol of male fertility. (The grape symbolizes female fertility.) The date is a symbol of abundance and contentment.

Fenugreek

Fenugreek is a natural deodorant that was also used in North Africa to increase the size and roundness of the female breast.[28] In Czechoslovakia, young women wore small bunches of fenugreek around their necks as a love charm.

Fig

The fig tree is a symbol of passion, fruitfulness, and life. The sacred fig tree (*ficus religiosa*) was venerated because it combined both male and female qualities. Its three-lobed leaf symbolized the male genitals, and became used to symbolically cover the genitals of nude statues. The breast-shaped fruit reminded people of the female principle, and was eaten to improve fecundity. In fact, the fig tree is sometimes referred to as the "many-breasted tree."

---

28. Pamela Allardice, *Love Potions: Charms and Other Romantic Notions* (Chippendale, Australia: Pan Macmillan Publishers, 1991), 23.

Grape

The grapevine is a traditional symbol of female fertility and passion. Bunches of grapes symbolize fecundity and sacrifice. They also symbolize sacrifice, as they produce blood-colored wine. In the Christian tradition, Jesus is sometimes symbolized as the "true vine," and the leaves represent his apostles. It can also symbolize the Christian church and its members.

Henbane

Henbane was a useful plant for magicians. Doctors and herbalists used it as an effective painkiller. The smoke given off when the plant was burned helped conjure spirits, and a faint picture of a future partner could sometimes be discerned in the smoke. Henbane was also used to create love potions.

Mandrake (Mandragora)

Mandrake has been considered a potent ingredient in love for so long that it is even mentioned in the first book of the Bible. The story of how Leah used mandrake to seduce Jacob can be found in Genesis 30:14–16. The ancient Egyptians called mandrake the "phallus of the field."

Mandrakes possess long, forked roots that make them look vaguely human-like. People believed that when it was pulled out of the ground, the mandrake would shriek so horribly that anyone who heard it would die in agony.

Mistletoe

Mistletoe is a parasitic plant that attaches itself to oak trees. The ancient Druids considered mistletoe to be a symbol of potency and fecundity, and used it in their fertility rites. This is because the white berries were thought to contain the tree's semen. Today, kissing under the mistletoe is a charming custom. However, it is important to burn the mistletoe on Twelfth Night. Tradition says the people who kissed beneath the mistletoe will quarrel within a year if this is not done.

Myrtle

In ancient times, myrtle was considered sacred to Aphrodite. Consequently, it came to symbolize love. Jewish people were the first to use it in bridal wreaths, often creating wreaths of roses and myrtle. Nowadays, a myrtle bridal wreath symbolizes virginity.

Oak

The oak tree has always been the most sacred tree in Europe and Scandinavia. Pliny the Elder (23–79 C.E.), the Roman author, wrote about the reverence the ancient Druids had for the oak. In Scandinavia, the oak was sacred to Thor, the great warrior god who gave his name to Thursday (Thor's day).

The oak plays a major role in folklore. The marriage oak was a tree that married couples danced around for good luck. This dates back to pagan wedding ceremonies that were held under oak trees.[29]

Olive

The olive tree symbolizes marriage, fertility, happiness, and abundance. A dove carrying an olive branch is a symbol of peace.

---

29. Anonymous, *Encyclopedia of Magic and Superstition* (London, UK: Octopus Books Limited, 1974), 218.

Orange

The orange blossom is a fertility symbol. In Japan, it symbolizes pure, innocent, perfect love.

Palm Tree

Because of its phallic shape, the palm tree symbolizes male virility. However, when it is depicted with dates, it is considered a female symbol of fertility and fruitfulness. The palm tree produces dates for many years. Because of this, it is sometimes considered a symbol of longevity.

Ancient people believed the palm tree created itself. Consequently, it was venerated as an androgynous symbol of the divine creative force. The Christians adopted the palm tree as a symbol of martyrdom. However, this may have been because they felt it represented the triumph of life over death. [30]

Peach

In China and Japan, the peach symbolizes marriage, as well as longevity, immortality, spring, and protection. The peach blossom is an emblem of virginity.

Pear

The pear has erotic connotations, possibly because its swollen shape resembles a breast. Another possibility is that its shape resembles the waist and buttocks. The pear is associated with Aphrodite, the Greek goddess of love.

---

30.   Elisabeth Goldsmith, *Ancient Pagan Symbols* (New York, NY: G. P. Putnam's Sons, Inc., 1929), 21.

Pomegranate

The pomegranate is one of the oldest symbols of love, fertility, and life. It is also associated with temptation. It is mentioned several times in The Song of Solomon. In China, it is one of the Three Blessed Fruits of Buddhism. In legend, when Persephone asked permission to return to the earth's surface, Hades gave her a pomegranate, which symbolized an eternal marriage. Once Persephone ate it, she was condemned to spend four months every year in the underworld with Hades. Pomegranates are supposed to have been born from the blood of Dionysus, the god of vegetation, wine, and ecstasy.

Rosemary

Rosemary has been used in charms for thousands of years to ensure success in love. It is a hardy, evergreen plant that symbolizes love, fidelity, and fertility. It was woven into bridal wreaths to ensure fidelity and happiness. Sprigs of rosemary were dunked into wine to ensure a happy marriage.

Sage

Sage has a long history as a herb that promotes love. Hippocrates suggested that all Greek women should drink sage wine to produce more children to replace the men who died in battle. According to English folklore, both men and women used sage as a love charm. If twelve leaves were plucked exactly at midnight on Midsummer Eve, the right lover would appear.

Tomato

For most of the nineteenth century, tomatoes were not considered fit to eat. They were called "love apples" and were considered symbols of love and fertility.[31]

Vervain

Virgil wrote that a mixture of vervain and frankincense would make even the coldest of people passionate. German brides still drink vervain tea to create fertility in the marriage.

Bernard's Experience

Bernard is an architect who has always loved oak trees.

"There was a grove of oak trees close to my home when I was growing up," he told me. "I spent a lot of time there, both on my own, and also playing with friends. I always considered oak trees to have personalities and souls. That's probably why I gave them names, and talked to them. Always when I was on my own, of course. Whenever I had a problem, I could go for a walk in the oak grove and come home feeling better. I didn't always have an answer, but I'd come back knowing I'd be able to handle it."

As a young man, Bernard took his girlfriend for a walk in the oak grove, and they both lost their virginity there.

"Maybe that's why I associate oak trees with love," Bernard said. He shrugged his shoulders. "But yet again, they'd always shown love to me, even when I was little."

Time passed, and Bernard fell in love several times before getting married. He left the family home, and he and his wife traveled

---

31.   Donald E. Dossey, *Holiday Folklore*, *Phobias and Fun*, (Los Angeles, CA: Outcomes Unlimited Press, Inc. 1992), 47.

extensively. Everywhere they settled, Bernard made sure there was at least one oak tree within easy walking distance. Three children arrived, and Bernard's career progressed. Everything seemed perfect, until one day he discovered his wife was having an affair.

"I was devastated," he told me. "It made a mockery of everything we'd built up together. I went home to my parents and spent a lot of time in my oak grove. The trees gave me comfort and advice. I blamed Cynthia for everything, but of course, it wasn't like that. I'd put all my energies into my career. She and the kids were well down on my list of priorities. I thought being a good provider was all I had to do. The trees gradually taught me some important lessons, including forgiveness. I returned to my family, and we've made some big changes. Things aren't perfect, but they're a lot better than they were. Cynthia and I are much more open about things. I'm a better listener than I used to be. I no longer bottle things up inside, either. I pause by the oak tree near our gate every day. It tells me when I'm on track, and when I'm not." Bernard smiled. "Isn't it funny that oak trees can save a marriage?"

CHAPTER SIX

Flowers

*F*lowers are rich in symbolism, and not surprisingly, much of this is concerned with love. After all, flowers are the reproductive organs of plants. The colors, shapes, and scents of flowers captivate the senses. A gift of flowers has always been considered a loving gesture. Tradition says that luck is increased if the bunch contains an odd number of flowers. The word "posy" originally meant a message of love.

Because the life span of a flower is so brief, flowers also symbolize the brevity of life. The symbolism of individual flowers varies in different parts of the world. This can also reflect the standards of certain societies. The Victorians disliked the peony, because they associated its rosy colors with loose morals. Halfway around the world, the Chinese revere the peony and consider it one of their five most important flowers. This is because it symbolizes fidelity, happiness, joy, and long life. It is also associated with love and feminine beauty. (The other four important flowers in China are the chrysanthemum, lotus, magnolia, and orchid.)[32]

Usually, the symbolism of different flowers is obvious. A white lily, not surprisingly, symbolizes purity and innocence. The heady, heavy perfume of the frangipani is a perfect symbol of sexual invitation.

Over the years, a language of flowers developed, in which every flower symbolized a thought or emotion. It began in the Orient, and was introduced to the West in the early eighteenth century by Lady Mary Wortley Montagu who learned the art while living in Turkey. Here are a few of her interpretations:

> Jonquil: Have pity on my passion.
> Rose: May you be pleased, and your sorrow become mine.
> Cinnamon: My fortune is yours.

Once you knew the language, you could read hidden meanings in a gift of a bouquet of flowers. A dahlia, for instance, is a symbol of danger. Consequently, a gift of dahlias could indicate that a secret, illicit affair is about to become public knowledge.

The language ultimately became extremely involved and complicated. A flower would have one meaning when worn

---

32. Richard Webster, *Feng Shui for Beginners* (St. Paul, MN, Llewellyn Publications, 1997), 103.

in the hair, another when it was worn over the heart, and yet another when it was held in the hand. If the flower were held upright, the news would be good. However, if it was held bloom downwards, the news was bad. The language also varied from country to country. The daisy, for example, meant "innocence" in England, but "I will think of it" in the United States.

The secret language of flowers was at its peak in Victorian times when people were not always able to express their thoughts and desires out loud. Symbolic meanings began to be attached to flowers in medieval times. William Shakespeare's audiences would have had no difficulty in understanding Ophelia's remarks to Laertes in *Hamlet*: "There's rosemary, that's for remembrance–pray you, love, remember. And there is pansies, that's for thoughts" (Act 4, scene 5, line 173).

Every month has been given a flower, which is intended to bring love, happiness, and good fortune to those born in it.

January: carnation, primrose
February: primrose
March: daffodil, violet
April: daisy
May: hawthorn, lily of the valley
June: rose, honeysuckle
July: water lily
August: gladioli, poppy
September: aster, convolvulus
October: dahlia
November: chrysanthemum
December: holly

Acacia

The acacia is a symbol of platonic love. Because it has both red and white flowers, it is also considered a symbol of immortality, or death and rebirth. In both Jewish and Christian traditions, the acacia symbolizes a good, moral life.

Clover

Clover represents vitality and energy because it is a fast-growing, vigorous plant. The three-leaf clover symbolizes the Trinity and protects the owner from harm. This belief dates back to the Middle Ages.

Traditionally, a four-leaf clover was believed to endow its owner with psychic ability. In the United States, a folk tradition says that whoever finds a four-leaf clover will shortly meet the person he or she will marry.

The four-leaf clover has been considered a potent source of good luck since the days of the ancient druids. They believed that it would help them see invisible negative spirits, which they would then be able to avoid. An old legend says Eve took a four-leaf clover with her when she left the Garden of Eden. Because of this, a four-leaf clover is believed to provide good luck to all couples.

Daisy

The common daisy has always been associated with love. Almost everyone has plucked the petals from a daisy, one by one, while reciting: "He/she loves me, he/she loves me not." It is also thought that you will receive a dream vision of your future lover by placing daisy roots under your pillow. A charming tradition says daisies were first formed from the tears of Mary Magdalene.

Dandelion

The dandelion has become associated with love and romance because of the ancient tradition of blowing the seeds off the top of a dandelion. The number of breaths it takes reveals the number of years it will be before you get married.

Forget-Me-Nots

Forget-me-nots have symbolized never-ending love for at least two thousand years. A sad, old Austrian legend tells the story of two lovers who walked by the Danube River and saw a blue flower bobbing up and down in the water. It was the day before they were to be married, and the girl sighed because the flower was drifting out of sight. Her gallant fiancé dived into the river to catch the flower. Unfortunately, he got caught in the strong undertow. Before he drowned, he managed to toss the flower ashore and call out: "My darling, forget me not!"

Traditionally, lovers give the forget-me-not to their partners on February 29th. This is to ensure that this day, which appears only once every four years, is remembered.

Heliotrope

There is a charming Greek myth that tells the story of the Heliotrope, a name that means "sun-follower" in Greek. A young maiden called Clytia fell in love with Helios, a god who pulled the sun across the heavens in his chariot. Unfortunately, Helios did not respond to the girl's affections, but Clytia continued gazing up at him every day until she finally died of a broken heart. The gods felt sorry for her, and rewarded her loyalty, love, and devotion by turning her into the purple flower. That is why the Heliotrope tracks the sun as it moves across the sky.

Hyacinth

This is not a flower for heterosexual couples to give to each other. However, it is an ideal flower for a gay man to present to a possible partner. This symbolism came about because of the brief relationship of Apollo and Hyacinthus. Hyacinthus was famous for his beauty. Unfortunately, both Apollo and Zephyrus, the god of the west wind, fell in love with him at the same time. One day, when Apollo and Hyacinthus were playing quoits, Zephyrus interfered by blowing at a quoit Apollo had thrown. The quoit struck Hyacinthus on the head and killed him. Apollo wept over the boy's body and changed Hyacinthus' blood into a flower.

Lily

The lily is an interesting flower, as it symbolizes purity and chastity to Christians, but was considered a symbol of eroticism and fertility by the Greeks. The pistil was considered highly phallic, and the pollen symbolized virility. Because of this, medieval priests removed the pistils and stamens of lilies to ensure modesty before using them in floral displays in churches.[33]

Greek mythology tells a story to explain the origin of both the Milky Way and the lily. Apparently, Zeus wanted his son Hercules to become a god. As Hercules was the result of a brief extra-marital affair, Hera, his wife, objected. Zeus asked Somnus, the god of sleep, to put her into a deep sleep. While

---

33. Anonymous, *Encyclopedia of Magic and Superstition*, (London, UK: Octopus Books Limited, 1974) 226.

Hera slept, Zeus put the baby to her breast. Hercules sucked so vigorously that the milk overflowed. Some flowed heavenwards and became the Milky Way. The milk that flowed on the ground became the white lily, the most popular emblem of purity. Aphrodite was annoyed at this. After all, she had been created from white sea foam. As a result, she gave the lily the large phallic pistil that so embarrassed medieval clerics.

A charming piece of Anglo-Saxon folklore tells how to foretell the sex of an unborn child. All you need to do is approach the expectant mother holding a lily in one hand and a rose in the other. If the woman chooses the rose, she will give birth to a girl. However, she will have a boy if she chooses the lily.

Lotus

As the lotus grows out of the mud, it symbolizes purity overcoming impurity. The lotus is one of eight precious things in Buddhism, and Buddha is frequently shown sitting on a lotus flower. In Tantric Buddhism, the stem symbolizes male genitalia and the red blossom symbolizes the female. This depicts Nirvana, or the "jewel in the lotus." Courtesans were frequently called "red lotus." If a man happens to come across a lotus blossom with a double style, it means he is with an old flame.[34] Lotus seeds symbolize fertility.

Marigold

Marigolds have been used as love charms throughout history. Sir James G. Frazer recorded how Balkan girls dug up earth that contained footprints of the person they had eyes on, and

---

34. Wolfram Eberhard, *A Dictionary of Chinese Symbols* (London, UK: Routledge and Kegan Paul Limited, 1986), 169.

placed it in a pot. They then potted a marigold in it as a symbol of their love. As the marigolds in the pot grew, so would the love of the other person.

In the eighteenth century, English girls would create a magic powder that apparently encouraged dreams relating to love and marriage. The formula is included in *Mother Bunch's Closet Newly Broken Open*, an anonymous chapbook of the time:

> *Take marigold flowers, a sprig of marjoram, thyme and a little wormwood; dry them before a fire, rub them to a powder, then sift it thro' a fine piece of lawn; simmer these with a small quantity of virgin honey in white wine over a slow fire; with this anoint your stomach, breast and lips lying down, and repeat these words thrice:*
>
> > *St. Luke, St. Luke, be kind to me;*
> >
> > *In dreams let me my true love see!*
>
> > *This said, hasten to sleep, and in the soft slumber of your night's repose, the very man whom you shall marry will appear before you, walking to and fro, near your bedside, very plain and visible to be seen.* [35]

Apparently, in your dream, a suitable man will approach you with a smile on his face. An unsuitable person will "be rude and uncivil with thee."

Narcissus

The narcissus is named after a handsome Greek youth who was loved by many, including Echo, who slowly pined away when her love was not returned. Finally, all that remained was

---

35. George Laurence Gomme (editor), *Mother Bunch's Closet Newly Broken Open, and the History of Mother Bunch of the West* (London, UK: Villon Society, 1885), 31.

a faint echo of her voice. Nemesis, the goddess of retribution, condemned Narcissus to spend the rest of his life admiring his own reflection in a pond. When he died, the gods turned him into the flower that bears his name.

There is another ancient Greek story about the narcissus. Pluto, lord of the underworld, was fascinated with Persephone, the beautiful daughter of Demeter, the goddess of marriage. Zeus helpfully offered to assist his fellow god by creating a new flower, the narcissus, to tempt Persephone away from her friends. The beautiful flower caught Persephone's eye and she walked toward it. As she did, the earth opened up beneath her, and a chariot drawn by two black horses rode out of it. Pluto, who was in the chariot, seized Persephone and carried her down to the underworld.

Pansy

The pansy was the first flower pierced by Cupid's arrow. It is known as "kiss me quick," making it a good choice for a young man hoping to captivate a lady. An old tradition says that if you place pansies over the eyes of someone who is asleep, he or she will fall in love with the first person they see when they wake up.

Rose

No flower symbolizes true love more than the rose. In ancient Greece, Aphrodite, the goddess of love, wore garlands of roses. The Greeks told a story of the love affair between Aphrodite and Adonis. In an attempt to prove his courage, Adonis went hunting and was killed by a savage boar. As he lay dying, a rose bush bloomed from his blood. As a result of this, the red rose has come to symbolize a love that not even death can extinguish.

Red roses are also believed to have sprouted from the blood of Jesus as he lay on the cross. Consequently, many Christians consider the red rose to symbolize the blood and wounds of Christ. Some people believe that the crown of thorns Jesus wore was made of rose briars, which adds to the symbolism.

The Roman expression "sub rosa" (under the rose) came from a garland or bouquet of roses that was hung over a dining table. This meant that everything that was said at the table should not be repeated later on. The Romans took this from a Greek myth. Because the rose was dedicated to Aphrodite, the goddess of love, her son, Eros, used roses to bribe Harpocrates, the god of silence, to keep quiet about his mother's numerous indiscretions.

The Romans grew enormous quantities of roses, mainly for their petals, which were used as carpets on significant occasions. The sheer volume of roses required was so immense that many Roman colonies began growing roses to help cater for this demand. Nero is believed to have spent four million sesterces on roses for just one banquet.[36] Roses were also sprinkled on couches and used to fill cushions. They were also turned into wine or attar. Rose petals were often placed on the surface of containers of wine. Famous shrines were decorated with garlands of roses, and athletes and dignitaries wore them at public games. Soldiers even planted rosebushes to celebrate returning home from war. At weddings, the bridal couple wore garlands of roses, because of their association with Venus, the Roman goddess of love and beauty.

The early church fathers loathed the rose because they associated it with the lust and debauchery they saw in the

---

36. E. Buckner Hollingsworth, *Flower Chronicles* (New Brunswick, NJ: Rutgers University Press, 1958), 30. In Nero's time, one sesterce would buy four donkeys.

Roman Empire. Consequently, many centuries passed before the rose could be associated with the Virgin Mary.

The color of the red rose symbolizes passion and eroticism. A white rose, on the other hand, symbolizes purity, chastity, and innocence. The yellow rose, which symbolized jealousy in Victorian times, is now a symbol of joy, happiness, and friendship.

John Aubrey (1626–97), the English diarist, wrote that grieving partners planted red roses on the graves of their dead lovers. They were supposed to look after the grave, and not remarry.[37]

The scent of the rose is considered an aphrodisiac. Cleopatra certainly knew this when she chose to entertain Mark Antony in a room liberally strewn with rose petals.

St. John's Wort

The St. John's Wort is a yellow flower that is believed to help couples conceive. The wife has to go naked in her garden on Midsummer's Eve (June 23rd) and pick a flower of St. John's Wort.

Tulip

The tulip symbolizes everlasting life. This comes from an old Persian legend about a prince who flung himself off a cliff after hearing that his wife had died. Tulips are believed to have grown from his blood.

Gardens

Flowers are normally found in gardens. Gardening is an extremely popular hobby with countless benefits for people who enjoy working with plants. Gardens can be incredibly sensual

---

37. John Aubrey, *Miscellanies* London, UK: William Barrett and Son, Limited, 1896, 87. (Originally published 1696. Many editions available.)

places with their beautiful colors, scents, and views. They consist of an idealized universe set within a frame formed from the walls or boundaries of the garden. The Garden of Eden was an earthly paradise, and the Song of Solomon was a poetic depiction of the walled gardens of ancient Persia. In King Solomon's poem, the garden is compared with a lover. The garden is a sexual paradise. The Arabic word for paradise is al-janna, "the garden."

Sexuality is a natural part of every garden. Plants, insects, and birds all reproduce there. Medieval gardens symbolized the womb, virginity, and secrecy.

Pamela's Experience

Pamela is now in her eighties. I got to know her many years ago because she spends almost every day tending her beautiful garden and chatting with passers-by. She talks to her flowers as she tends them, and says that as a result of this, she has no stress or worries in her life. I am constantly amazed that, no matter what the time of year, Pamela always has something flowering in her garden.

Pamela's love for growing flowers is obvious, but she also considers them a symbol of universal love.

"I plant with love," she says. "And then, once they've grown, they send out love to the world. You can see that in the smiles of the people who look at them. I believe my garden brightens the lives of a few people. However, their cheerfulness improves the lives of the people they interact with, and so it goes on and on—I like to see it as waves of love."

"That means you see flowers as symbols of love?" I asked.

Pamela beamed. "Of course. You've just got to look at a flower to know it symbolizes love."

CHAPTER SEVEN

Minerals

$\mathcal{S}$tones of various sorts have always been used as amulets and charms. The fertility stones used by gypsies in Europe are a good example. These are small stones that approximate the torso of a pregnant woman who is about to give birth. Gypsy sorcerers give these stones to young girls to help them conceive. Frequently, these stones are engraved with magical symbols, such as a serpent for protection and guidance, and a five-pointed star, showing that the owner of the stone is a daughter of the sun. The name of the place where the woman will conceive is sometimes inscribed on the stone in code form, as is the place where she will give birth.

Gemstones have a long history and a large number of gemstones have gained romantic connotations. Ruby denotes passion, for instance, while emerald offers sincerity. Amethyst relates to Venus and romantic love. Diamond denotes the permanence of marriage.

Amethyst

The deep purple color of the amethyst is believed to symbolize eternal love. In the days of chivalry, a gift of a heart-shaped amethyst set in silver "was said to confer the greatest possible earthly happiness on the pair who would be blessed with good fortune for the remainder of their lives."[38]

Legend says that St. Valentine wore an amethyst ring with the figure of Cupid engraved on it. An unknown eleventh century German author wrote: "an amethyst owned by a man attracts to him the love and affection of noble women, and protects him from thieves."[39]

Aquamarine

Jewelry containing aquamarine is believed to ensure a good marriage, and a stable home and family life. It is considered highly auspicious if a groom presents aquamarine to his wife on their wedding day.

---

38. William Thomas and Kate Pavitt, *The Book of Talismans, Amulets and Zodiacal Gems* (Originally published 1914. Republished by Kessinger Publishing Company, Whitefish, MT, n.d.), 275.

39. Harriet Keith Fobes, *Mystic Gems* (Boston, MA: Richard G. Badger, 1924), 23.

Beryl

Beryl is worn to attract love, and to protect the wearer from relationships that will not last. It can also be given to the person you love as a symbol of your adoration.

Diamond

An old story says Cupid's arrows have diamond tips. This is not surprising, as the diamond is the gemstone that says love better than all the others. However, the cult of diamond engagement rings goes back not much more than five hundred years. One of the first people to use "a ring set with a diamond" was Archduke Maximilian of Austria, in 1477. When he presented a diamond engagement ring to Mary of Burgundy, a celebrated beauty of her day, she agreed to marry him.[40] The custom became popular and today it is estimated that 70 percent of brides in the United States wear a diamond engagement ring. It takes their future husbands, on average, two months salary to buy it.[41]

Despite the popularity of the diamond, it has not always brought luck with it. The famous Hope diamond, a 44.4-carat greenish-blue stone, is believed to have brought bad luck to everyone who owned it. It is now in the Smithsonian Institute in Washington, D.C. It was purchased in India by Jean Baptiste Tavernier (1605–1689), a famous French precious gem merchant, in 1642. He sold it to King Louis XIV in 1668. One hundred and twenty years later, Marie Antoinette wore it. It disappeared during the French Revolution, but was found again and

40. George Frederick Kunz, *Rings for the Finger* (Philadelphia, PA: J. B. Lipppincott Company, 1917), 234–235.
41. Denny Lee and Josh Stoneman, *Symbols of Love* (New York, NY: Assouline Publishing, Inc., 2002), 40.

sold to the English banker, Henry Philip Hope, for $90,000. Later owners included Jacques Colet, who committed suicide, Prince Ivan Kanitovitsky, who was murdered, Sultan Abdul Hamed, who was dethroned, and Simon Montharides who lost his entire family in an accident. Between 1911 and 1947, Mrs. Evelyn Walsh McLean, an American, owned it. Her husband, son, and daughter all died shortly after she bought it.

But what about the ill luck this stone is supposed to possess? Marie Antoinette died on the guillotine, the Sultana of Abdul Hamid was shot by her husband while wearing it, and Habid Bey, another owner, drowned at sea. Even a French broker who was involved in handling the sale of the stone met an untimely death.[42]

A diamond ring is supposed to mean forever, but this is not always the case. The marriage between the film stars Richard Burton and Elizabeth Taylor lasted only seven years after he spent one million dollars on a 69.42-carat diamond.

Emerald

The ancient Egyptians called the emerald "the lover's stone" because it was believed to enhance love and fertility. It was also supposed to cure impotence and ensure that lovers remained true to each other. If the wife wore an emerald, she would remain chaste and faithful while her husband was away.

In fact, the emerald was supposed to ensure that by breaking into pieces if the wife was untrue. Albertus Magnus told a story about King Bela of Hungary (1235–1270) and his unfaith-

---

42. Michael Weinstein, *The World of Jewel Stones* (London, UK: Sir Isaac Pitman and Sons, Limited, 1959), 44.

ful queen. When he returned home from an expedition, King Bela embraced his wife. At that moment, his precious emerald ring broke into three pieces, revealing his wife's indiscretions.[43]

Lodestone

The lodestone is magnetite, or magnetic iron ore. Because it is magnetic, it was credited with attracting positive qualities, such as good luck, prosperity, strength, and love. The French name for the lodestone is *aimant*, which comes from *aimer*, to love. In Sanskrit, it is called *chumbaka*, which means the kisser. The Chinese call is *t'su shi*, the loving stone.

The Roman poet Claudian (340–410) wrote a poem about a festival in which an iron statue of the god Mars and a lodestone statue of the goddess Venus were drawn to each other. The Romans believed that lodestone enhanced a marriage and ensured that the love remained inside the relationship.

Lodestone is also believed to possess aphrodisiacal qualities. It was thought a woman would be instantly ready for love when she lay down on a bed that also contained a lodestone. A man's virility is increased if he soaks a lodestone in oil and then rubs himself with it.[44] This was also done in ancient Assyria. In addition to this, the woman would rub an iron powder on herself to increase her desirability. Thus prepared, the man and the woman would be sufficiently magnetized to enjoy their lovemaking.[45]

---

43. George Frederick Kunz, *The Curious Lore of Precious Stones* (Philadelphia, PA: J. B. Lippincott Company, 1913), 78.

44. Bill Harris, *The Good Luck Book* (Owings Mills: Ottenheimer Publishers, 1996), 108.

45. Scott Cunningham, *Cunningham's Encyclopedia of Crystal, Gem & Metal Magic* (St. Paul, MN: Llewellyn Publications, 1988), 163.

In 1600, Gianpaolo Osio seduced an Italian nun called Virginia Maria de Leyva after placing a lodestone in her mouth. In her confession, Virginia said that "some diabolical force" had made her submit to Gianpaolo's advances.[46]

In the past, prostitutes used to rub themselves with lodestones to attract customers. Recently, I was told that some prostitutes in Mexico still do this.

Pearl

The pearl is a particularly feminine stone, symbolizing grace, charm, and beauty. It is believed to help infertile couples have children, but is also believed to create tears. The origin of the superstition about tears is an interesting one. People noticed that pearls were created when the oyster tried to obtain relief from an irritation caused by a foreign substance that had penetrated the shell. The suffering and pain of the oyster create the beautiful pearl. The pearl is associated with Venus, the goddess of love, as both came from the sea and are capable of instantly captivating others.

Rose Quartz

Quartz is a compound of silica and oxygen and is one of the earth's most abundant minerals. Rose quartz is often referred to as the "love stone" or "heart stone." It is frequently used to help balance the heart chakra. It is also said to enhance the person's ability to receive and express love, both romantic and platonic.

---

46.   Edward S. Gifford, *The Charms of Love* (London, UK: Faber and Faber Limited, 1963), 60.

Ruby

The fiery red color of the ruby means that it has always been associated with passion and love. It was considered a powerful aphrodisiac that could inflame lovers with uncontrollable passion. They
were also supposed to be able to communicate clairvoyantly with
their owners, particularly about affairs of the heart. Catherine of
Aragon was supposed to have owned a ruby that gradually lost its
color as King Henry VIII lost interest in her.[47]

Selenite (Moonstone)

Selenite is a soft stone with a pearly luster. In his classic work, *De
Lapidibus*, Marbode, Bishop of Rennes (1035–1123), wrote that
selenite reconciles problems between lovers and brings them
closer together.[48] Selenite also symbolizes good fortune in love.[49]

Metals

Precious metals, such as silver and gold, have been used in the creation of various forms of body adornment for thousands of years.
Craftspeople have made jewelry and other objects to beautify the
body for 40,000 years.[50] Gold was discovered more than 5,000
years ago, and immediately became prized and popular in the
manufacture of jewelry. For most of its history, jewelry has been
worn as a sign of rank, or to act as an amulet or lucky charm.

---

47. William Thomas and Kate Pavitt, *The Book of Talismans, Amulets and Zodiacal
Gems* (Whitefish, MT: Kessinger Publishing Company), 252–253.
48. There are several translations of *De Lapidibus* in English. The one I have is by C.
W. King (1870), which is included in *Gems in Myth, Legend, and Lore* by Bruce
G. Knuth (Thornton, CO: Jewelers Press, 1999), 211–226.
49. William Thomas and Kate Pavitt, *The Book of Talismans, Amulets and Zodiacal
Gems* (London, UK: Rider & Company, Limited, 1914), 183.
50. Encyclopaedia Britannica, *Macropaedia 10,* (Chicago, IL: Encyclopaedia Britannica, Inc., 15th ed., 1983), 164.

A few metals have become associated with love and romance:

Copper

Copper is associated with the planet Venus, and is frequently used for healing and for attracting love. It can also be used to attract money. Any form of copper jewelry, such as a bracelet, can be worn to attract love. Precious stones, such as emerald, make the jewelry even more effective.

Gold

Gold is associated with the sun. It symbolizes power, status, and wealth. Gold provides symbolic protection, while at the same time granting confidence and strength. It is considered masculine and has been used to help men suffering from sexual dysfunction. As it gives enormous personal power, gold has an aphrodisiac effect on both sexes.

Silver

Silver is associated with the Moon. It symbolizes the emotions, intuition, dreams, protection, and love. Silver jewelry, especially objects that also contain precious stones, can be used to attract love. A silver ring, with an attractive stone mounted on it, is all that is required. Some people find it hard to wear silver at the time of the Full Moon. This is because silver has a strong effect on the emotions. If silver affects you this way, either do not wear silver at the time of the Full Moon, or wear some gold as well to provide balance.

Rings

Rings have been associated with love and romance since at least
Roman times.[51] Rings have no beginning and no end. Consequently, they symbolize eternity. This association can also be
interpreted as enduring love and a happy, stable marriage.

The custom of placing the wedding ring on the Apollo finger of the left hand possibly came from the Egyptian belief that
a nerve ran directly from this finger to the heart. However,
the wedding ring has been placed on different fingers at different times. During the reign of George II, many people wore
the wedding ring on their thumb. Samuel Butler (1612–1680)
referred to this in his satire against Puritanism, *Hudibras*:

> *Others were for abolishing*
> *That tool of matrimony, a ring*
> *With which the unsanctify'ed bridegroom*
> *Is marry'd only to a thumb.*[52]

The Claddagh Ring

In Ireland, the symbol of friendship, loyalty, and love is the
Claddagh ring. This is a ring consisting of two hands holding a
heart, which wears a crown. The two hands symbolize friendship, the heart love, and the crown loyalty. The origin of this
ring is not known, but the Irish love good stories and have a
charming tale to explain where it came from.

---

51. George Frederick Kunz, *Rings for the Finger* (Philadelphia, PA: J. B. Lippincott
    Company, 1917), 193.
52. Samuel Butler, Hudibras. This lengthy, burlesque satirical poem makes fun of
    Puritanism. It was published in three parts, in 1663, 1664, and 1678. Hudibras
    was extremely popular at the time and, although much of it sounds quaint today,
    can still be read for enjoyment. This poem was a favorite of King Charles II.

A young girl called Margaret Joyce lived in Galway in the sixteenth century. One day while washing clothes, she met an elderly Spanish merchant. He fell in love, and after marrying her, took her back to Spain where he promptly died. Margaret, now a wealthy widow, returned to Ireland, where she met Oliver Og Ffrench, the mayor of Galway. They married in 1596. While he was away on a lengthy business trip, Margaret decided to spend some of her money on an unusual hobby. She began building numerous stone bridges all over Connaught. Margaret regularly inspected the workmanship, and one day, while sitting beside a half-erected bridge, a large eagle dropped a golden ring into her lap. This was the first Claddagh ring.

A more believable story is also told about Richard Joyce. In 1675, Richard Joyce was on a ship heading toward the West Indies when it was captured by pirates. Richard was sold into slavery, and was bought by an Algerian goldsmith. He worked for him for almost fifteen years, until William III sent an ambassador to Algiers demanding the release of all British slaves. During his time as a slave, Richard had learned the art of working with precious metals. When he returned to Ireland, he set himself up as a goldsmith and achieved enormous success. Much of his work still survives, and these include many Claddagh rings.

Claddagh rings became treasured heirlooms that were passed down from mother to daughter, and sometimes grandmother to granddaughter. Claddagh rings are still popular today. Women receive them as gifts from their mothers, grandmothers, boyfriends, and other close friends. Men receive them from their girlfriends, fathers, or for serving as best man at a wedding.[53]

Gareth's Experience

Gareth married when he was twenty years old. His wife was two years younger and pregnant. The marriage lasted ten years, but in reality, had finished several years earlier. Gareth revelled in his new freedom and spent the next few years trying to do all the things he thought he had missed out on by being married.

"It was great for a while," he told me. "But it wasn't fulfilling. I felt empty all the time, and used to do more and more crazy things to feel alive. One night I got arrested for being drunk. It wasn't much fun waking up in a police cell. But it turned out to be the wake-up call I needed.

"A few days later, I was in a coffee shop, feeling sorry for myself. I must have looked pretty bad, too, as a guy who was there came over and started talking to me. I thought he was going to spout religion at me, but instead he talked about setting goals and having a dream. When he got up to go, he gave me a tiny amethyst. I didn't want to accept it, as it looked valuable. I thought it must have been something precious he carried around with him, like a lucky charm. However, he insisted. He put it in the palm of my hand, closed my fingers over it, and tapped my fist three times with his forefinger. 'That stone means love,' he told me. 'Universal love. The love I have for you and everyone

---

53.   Malachy McCourt, *The Claddagh Ring* (Philadelphia, PA: Running Press Book Publishers, 2003), 107.

else on this planet. It also means that special love between two people. Carry it with you and see what happens. Promise?'

"I still get a tingly feeling in my spine when I think about that chance encounter. His words were perfect for me at that moment. I just wish I'd thanked him properly. I remember mumbling something. He just smiled at me, and left.

"I did as he told me. I carried the stone around with me. I didn't even know it was an amethyst at the time. I got a small bag to keep it in, as I was scared I'd lose it. Each night I carefully put it beside my bed. It must have been a few months later when I realized how much better my life was. I was laughing about something, and suddenly thought it was the first time I'd laughed since leaving my ex. It occurred to me I was getting on better with everyone. Of course, the best thing was meeting Leigh, who is now my partner.

"I'd met her a couple of years earlier, but she didn't like me then. I was still married at that time, and probably came across as angry and unhappy. I was in the supermarket one day and she came up to talk to me. She said she could tell I was a different person. Women's intuition, I guess. Anyway, we hit it off right away, and now we're a couple."

Gareth proudly showed me his amethyst. It was less than half an inch in diameter, yet Gareth held it as if it was a precious diamond.

"I wouldn't tell everyone this," he told me. "But this amethyst turned my life around."

he invention of numbers enabled people to count and measure. However, almost simultaneously, they were also used for spiritual and metaphysical purposes. Four thousand years ago, the ancient Sumerians tried to explain the entire universe mathematically.

The belief that numbers have magical and symbolic significance is extremely old. Mathematical philosophers in Babylon and Greece believed that numbers could reveal the mysteries of life. The ancient Hindus believed numbers were the building blocks of the universe. The Aztecs associated each number with a god, direction, quality, and color.[54]

Numerology is one of the oldest occult sciences. It is so old that Pythagoras (c. 580 B.C.E.–c. 500 B.C.E.), the Greek philosopher and mathematician, is credited with modernizing it more than 2,500 years ago. He considered the universe to be a balance of opposites. Odd numbers, for instance, were considered to be masculine and active, while even numbers were feminine and passive.

Numerology has changed and developed over the last few thousand years, and numerology today has little in common with the numerology practiced by the Sumerians or the members of Pythagoras' mystery school. In fact, numerology as we know it today is not much more than one hundred years old.[55]

Your Most Important Numbers

Although your numerological chart contains most, if not all, of the numbers, four are considered especially important. These are your Life Path, Expression, Soul Urge, and Day of Birth.

Life Path

Your Life Path reveals your purpose in life, and represents about 40 percent of your makeup. It is derived from your full date of birth, reduced down to a single digit. Unfortunately, there are two exceptions. In the process of reducing the numbers down to a single digit, you stop if the numbers reduce to

---

54. Jack Tresidder, *Dictionary of Symbols* (San Francisco, CA: Chronicle Books, 1998), 146.
55. Matthew Oliver Goodwin, *Numerology: The Complete Guide, Volume 1* (North Hollywood, CA: Newcastle Publishing Company, Inc., 1981), 4.

either an 11 or 22. This is because these are Master Numbers. Here are two examples, one involving a Master Number:

12 (month)

9 (day)

1967 (year)

These numbers are added together, and reduced to a single digit: 12 + 9 + 1967 = 1988. 1 + 9 + 8 + 8 = 26. And 2 + 6 = 8. This person has a Life Path number of 8.

2 (month)

29 (day)

1944 (year)

1 + 9 + 7 + 5 = 22. As the 22 is not reduced further, this person has a Life Path number of 22.

Expression

Your Expression number reveals your natural abilities. In numerology, it represents 30 percent of your makeup. Your Expression number is derived from the letters in your full name at birth. These are converted into numbers and reduced down to a single digit or a Master Number. The first person to use numerology in this way was Cornelius Agrippa. Here is the chart he devised:

1	2	3	4	5	6	7	8	9
A	B	C	D	E	F	G	H	I
J	K	L	M	N	O	P	Q	R
S	T	U	V	W	X	Y	Z	

Let's work out the Expression number of an imaginary person called Elizabeth Mary Smith. We start by converting each letter into a number. We then add them up, and finally reduce them to a single digit (or Master Number).

ELIZABETH MARY SMITH
5 3 9 8 1 2 5 2 8 4 1 9 7 1 4 9 2 8

43 21 24

7 3 6

$7 + 3 + 6 = 16$, and $1 + 6 = 7$

Elizabeth has an Expression number of 7.

Soul Urge

The Soul Urge number reveals your inner motivation, your heart's desire. It shows what the person desires from life. The Soul Urge represents 20 percent of the person's makeup. It is derived from the vowels in the person's full name at birth reduced down to a single digit (or a Master Number). The Soul Urge is complicated in that the letter "Y" is sometimes classed as a consonant, but at other times can be a vowel. If it is pronounced, as in "Yolande," it is considered a consonant. If it acts as vowel, as in "Daryl," or is not pronounced, as in "Kaye," it is classed as a vowel.

The "Y" in "Mary," Elizabeth's middle name, is classed as a vowel.

ELIZABETH MARY SMITH

5 9 1 5 1 7 9

20 8 9

2 8 9 and $2 + 8 + 9 = 19$, $1 + 9 = 10$, and $1 + 0 = 1$.

Elizabeth's Soul Urge is 1.

Day of Birth

The day of the month you were born on is responsible for the final 10 percent of your makeup. (In fact, this is not totally correct, as numerology involves much more than these four numbers. These percentages show the relative weighting of each number in your makeup. Your Life Path makes up 40 percent. Consequently, it is four times more influential than your day of birth.) The day of birth has an influence on the other three numbers, and can be considered an additional, but less important, lesson than that provided by the Life Path.

Again, the day of birth is reduced down to a single digit, except for the Master Numbers. People born on the 11th, 22nd, and 29th of the month have a Master Number in their day of birth. (29 reduces to an 11.)

Interpretations For Each Number

Here are the basic meanings of each number:

One

One symbolizes independence and attainment. People with this number as one of their four main numbers have a strong desire to stand on their own two feet and to achieve something worthwhile.

Two

Two symbolizes harmony and cooperation. People with a two in their chart can harmonize and balance difficult situations. They are gentle, loving, adaptable, and considerate.

Three

Three symbolizes creativity and the joys of life. People with a three in their chart need to express themselves in some sort of way, ideally creatively. They are positive, optimistic, and enthusiastic.

Four

Four symbolizes system, order, and hard work. People with a four in their chart are capable, well organized, and prepared to work hard to achieve their goals. They can be rigid and stubborn. They need to work within the limits they find.

Five

Five symbolizes freedom, variety, and change. People with a five in their chart are versatile, adventurous, and positive. They need to use their freedom wisely, rather than scattering their talents over too wide an area.

Six

Six symbolizes love, as well as home and family responsibilities. People with a six in their chart are frequently responsible for far more than their fair share. They are the people others are attracted to when they need a shoulder to lean on. Six is also a creative number.

Seven

Seven symbolizes wisdom and understanding. According to the Bible, God made the world in six days and rested on the seventh. People with a seven in their chart need time on their own to learn, to understand, and to develop spiritually. Seven utilizes a different approach to life that can make people with this number appear remote and hard to get to know.

Eight

Eight symbolizes money and material freedom. People with an eight in their chart will work hard to achieve their financial goals. They can be generous once they have achieved their financial goals. They are stubborn, rigid, self-centered, and ambitious.

Nine

Nine symbolizes humanitarianism and universal love. People with a nine in their chart are generous, caring, and frequently selfless. They experience great pleasure from giving to others.

Master Numbers

Eleven and twenty-two are called Master Numbers. They are on a higher spiritual level than the other numbers. People with them have greater potential than those without them. However, these people are generally not aware of that, especially early on in life, and are held back by nervous tension and self-doubts. They are usually at their peak late in life, once they have learned how to handle the enormous potential of their Master Number.

Eleven

Eleven symbolizes idealism, intuition, and illumination. People with an eleven in their chart are idealistic, impractical dreamers who have visions of a perfect world. Once they become aware of their special capabilities, and learn to keep their feet on the ground, they have unlimited potential to achieve their goals.

Twenty-Two

Twenty-two is frequently known as the Master Builder. This is because people with this number in their charts have the potential to harness the idealism of the eleven, with a practical, pragmatic approach, to achieve goals that would daunt most others.

Progression of the Numbers

The numbers can be looked at in different ways. Each number can be considered to be the opposite of the number that precedes it. Six, for instance, symbolizes responsibility, while five symbolizes freedom.

I prefer to see the numbers as a logical progression. One (independence) is followed by two (cooperation). Three (creative self-expression) is followed by four (limitations, hard work). Five (freedom, variety) is followed by six (home and family responsibilities). Seven (spirituality) is followed by eight (material freedom). Nine (humanitarianism) is followed by eleven (idealism, impracticality).

Harmonizing the Numbers

Your Life Path, Expression, Soul Urge, and Day of Birth numbers may all be different. However, it is possible for two, three, or even four of the numbers to be the same. When this occurs, the person is likely to have difficulties early on in life harmonizing and balancing the number that has been doubled, tripled, or quadrupled.

Some groups of numbers harmonize easily. Three, six, and nine are all creative numbers. Someone with all of these numbers in his or her makeup will have considerable creative potential and be highly original.

One, four, and eight is another group that harmonizes well. Someone with these numbers would do well in business.

No matter what numbers make up your Life Path, Expression, Soul Urge, and Day of Birth, the combination of them is a symbol of you, numerologically speaking.

Compatibility

Numerology is a useful way to test your compatibility with someone else. Generally speaking, you will get on better with someone who shares one of your four main numbers. If you have a six Life Path, for instance, you would get on with people who also had a six as one of their four main numbers: their Life Path, Expression, Soul Urge, or day of birth. The presence of this number in common gives you both a contact point. You will look at the world in much the same way, and will share similar views. A close friendship or romantic relationship could develop as a result.

The closest relationships occur when two people have the same Soul Urge number. However, this does not necessarily ensure a long-lasting relationship. All relationships need to be looked after. If someone fails to nurture, support, and love his or her partner, the relationship will not last, no matter how good the numerological nuances of the names may be.

The Planes of Expression

Everyone on this planet contains a body, mind, heart, and spirit. Two people might share the same Soul Urge number, but if they operate on totally different levels on the Planes of Expression, they will have problems. If one person predominately uses his or her mind, but has a partner who primarily works on emotions (the heart plane), it is likely they will experience difficulties. Likewise, someone who works mainly on the physical (common-sense) plane will find it hard to communicate with people who operate mainly from the mind (reasoning), heart (emotional), or spirit (intuitional) levels.

The Planes of Expression are determined from the numbers relating to each letter of your full name at birth:

The Physical Level (Body) 4 and 5

The Mental Level (Mind) 1 and 8

The Emotional Level (Heart) 2, 3, and 6

The Intuitional Level (Spirit) 7 and 9

Here is how Elizabeth Mary Smith operates:

Physical (E, E, M, M) 4

Mental (Z, A, H, A, S, H) 6

Emotional (L, B, T) 3

Intuitional (I, R, Y, I, T) 5

Elizabeth is fortunate in that she can operate on any level. However, the two strongest are the Mental and Intuitional Planes. In a moment of crisis, she is likely to use these methods of expression, in preference to emotional or physical. Here is another example:

FRANK ORVILLE FOX
69 1 5 2 6 949335 6 66

PHYSICAL (N, V, E) 3

MENTAL (A) 1

EMOTIONAL (F, K, O, L, L, F, O, X) 8

INTUITIONAL (R, R, I) 3

In a moment of crisis, Frank would always express himself emotionally as this plane of expression is so much higher than the others.

Frank and Elizabeth would have problems in a relationship, no matter how harmonious their four main numbers were. This is because whenever anything went wrong, their responses would be totally different.

Numbers as Symbols

Many of the early fathers of the Christian Church were fascinated with the symbolism of numbers and how they were used in the Bible. St. Jerome noticed that the five Books of the Law, the eight Books of the Prophets, and the nine Books of the Hagiographa totalled twenty-two, the numbers of letters in the Hebrew alphabet. He also discovered that there are five double letters in the Hebrew alphabet and also five double books in the Bible: two Samuels, two Kings, two Chronicles, two Ezras (Ezra and Nehemiah), and two Jeremiahs (Jeremiah and Lamentations).[56]

The Jewish people consider their alphabet to be of divine origin, and a great deal of symbolism is attached to it. The Jewish kabbalah uses number symbolism extensively.

Numbers are highly symbolic on their own, but are usually linked with other forms of symbolism. Seven, for instance, is connected with the seven visible planets, and twelve is associated with the signs of the zodiac.

---

56. Ernest Busenbark, Symbols, *Sex, and the Stars: In Popular Beliefs* (New York, NY: The Truth Seeker Company, Inc., 1949), 245–246.

Four of the numbers are especially related to the themes of love and romance. They are two, three, five, and six.

Here are the symbolic meanings of each number:

One

One symbolizes individuality. One stands all by itself. Consequently, it is not a symbol of love and romance, though it can represent someone both before and after a relationship. A single bed belongs to someone who sleeps alone, by choice or circumstance. In feng shui, a bed that has a long side against a wall symbolizes someone who does not want a partner. A single bed with a long side placed against a wall, not only looks like the numeral one, but clearly shows the subconscious desire of the person who sleeps there to be on his or her own.

Two

Two is considered a feminine, maternal number. It symbolizes a dualistic world, with day and night, heaven and earth, water and earth, and yin and yang. The ancient Egyptians used lucky amulets in the shape of two fingers. They were reputed to bring good luck.[57] Cornelius Agrippa considered two to be the number of marriage. He wrote: "It (two) is also called the number of charity and mutual love, of marriage, and society, as it is said by the Lord, two shall be one flesh."[58]

---

57. Bill Harris, *The Good Luck Book* (Owings Mills, MD: Ottenheimer Publishers, 1996), 121.

58. Henry Cornelius Agrippa, *Three Books of Occult Philosophy,* edited by Donald Tyson (St. Paul, MN: Llewellyn Publications, 1993), 245.

Three

Three has always been considered a positive number in symbolism, mythology, legend, folklore, and religion. Three appears commonly in different religions. The Hindus had Brahma, Vishnu, and Shiva. The Egyptians had Isis, Osiris, and Horus. The Greeks had the three brothers, Zeus, Poseidon, and Hades. In Christianity, three is the number of the Trinity. Three also appears numerous times in the New Testament. These include the three crosses at Golgotha, the Resurrection after three days, and the three denials of Peter.

Three also symbolizes the family unit of mother, father, and child. The ancient Romans wore rings engraved with three ravens to attract love and romance.

Four

The number four contains a great deal of symbolism. It relates to the square, which conveys honesty and integrity. This may be related to solidity. In Pythagorean numerology, one relates to a point, two to a line, three to a surface, and four to a solid. It also relates to the four elements, the four winds, the four cardinal directions, and even the four evangelists (Matthew, Mark, Luke, and John), the four rivers that flow from the Tree of Life in Eden, and the four stages of life (childhood, youth, maturity, and old age).

Five

The Greeks associated five with Aphrodite, the goddess of love and marriage. This symbolism may have come originally from Mesopotamia, as they used a five-pointed star to symbolize Ishtar, their goddess of love. Ishtar's planet was Venus.

The number five symbolized marriage to the Pythagoreans. This is because it was the sum of the two opposites, two and three. As two was considered feminine, and three masculine, it is not surprising that five came to symbolize a permanent relationship between a man and a woman. (Number one symbolized unity to the Pythagoreans and was not considered a number. Consequently, three was considered the first male number.)

Six

The number six symbolizes union, love, and family. This association may have originally come from the Star of David symbol, a hexagram that contains two overlapping triangles, one pointing upward and the other down. The upward pointing triangle symbolizes fire, air, and masculine energy. The downward pointing triangle symbolizes water, earth, and female energy.

Six is also the product of the first male number and the first female number ($3 \times 2 = 6$). The combination of male and female frequently produces children, which is why six symbolizes family.

Seven

Seven has always been considered a sacred, magical number. This probably dates back to the seven planets (Sun, Moon, Venus, Mars, Mercury, Jupiter, and Saturn) that the ancients were familiar with. Another influence in this would have been the four seven-day phases that make up the lunar calendar.

There are numerous references to the number seven in the Bible, starting with God resting on the seventh day (Genesis 2:2). In Hinduism, the world mountain has seven faces. Seven is the number of perfection in Islam, which is why pilgrims walk around the Ka'aba at Mecca seven times. They also have seven earths, seas, heavens, hells, and doorways to Paradise. Seven was associated with protection and childbirth in Arabia. There were also seven Pillars of Wisdom, seven deadly sins, seven hills of Rome, and, in Japan, seven Gods of Luck.

Eight

Eight is a symbol of rebirth and renewal. This is why baptismal fonts are usually eight-sided. Seven is often considered the number of completion, which means eight is the number of new starts. Eight also symbolizes the four cardinal directions, along with the four intermediary ones. The Star of Bethlehem is often shown with eight points. In Hinduism, Vishnu has eight arms. In Chinese Taoism and Japanese Shintoism, there are eight Immortals.

An eight-pointed star originally symbolized the Roman goddess Venus, with lines joining each opposite point. This symbol was also the Gnostic sign of creation.

Nine

The number nine is an important number in most traditions. For the Hebrews, it symbolized truth. Christians had nine choirs of angels, possibly because they saw nine as the symbol of order within order. Odin, the Norse god of knowledge and wisdom, hanged himself on Yggdrasil, the World Tree, for nine days and nights. He was then pierced with a spear, and his blood created the first runic symbols.

Eleven

Eleven is a master number in numerology and symbolizes mastery in the physical dimension. It is the sum of five and six, which relate to the microcosm and macrocosm, or Heaven and

Earth. In Africa, it is related to fertility. St. Augustine didn't like the number eleven as he associated it with sin. Ten, in his mind, was perfect, which meant that eleven related to over-indulgence and excess. However, for other Christians, eleven related to the faithful apostles.

Twenty-Two

Twenty-two is the second master number in numerology, and symbolizes mastery of the mental and emotional dimensions. Twenty-two is also the sum total of all the letters in the Hebrew alphabet. The sacred texts of the Zoroastrians, the Avesta, were written in books of twenty-two chapters. They also had twenty-two sacred prayers. In Christianity, the Revelation of St. John contains twenty-two chapters. There are also twenty-two major arcana cards in the Tarot, and twenty-two paths that connect the ten sephiroth in the Tree of Life.

Jeremy's Experience

Jeremy came to one of my first numerology classes, more than thirty years ago. I remembered him well, as he sat in the front row, and used shorthand to record everything I said. I recently met him again at a New Age festival, and was interested to hear how he'd used numerology to attract his partner.

"I remember you saying that when two people have the same Soul Urge number, they live for each other," he told me. "My Soul Urge number was nine, so I created a collage using that number. I got sheets of colored paper, and cut out the number nine in different sizes and colors. I then glued them all over a large piece of cardboard. I hung this on my bedroom wall, so I could see it last thing at night and first thing in the morning. Then I got the idea of carrying a nine around with me. I made a small one out of paper and had it laminated. I kept it in my wallet. It worked like one of your silent affirmations. Each time I saw it, I remembered I was telling the universe to send me the right person.

"Actually, it took quite a while, but that was partly my fault. I went overseas for a few months, and then came back and looked after my sick aunt until she died. So I was out of circulation for about a year. Anyway, one Saturday morning I made myself a coffee. While it was brewing, I pulled the nine out of my wallet and was looking at it. I was about to pour the coffee when the doorbell went. I went to the door, and there was Tom. He was supposed to be going next door, but came to my house by mistake.

"It's amazing. You'd have thought we'd always known each other. He could smell the coffee, so I invited him in. I did his numbers, and almost died when I discovered he had a nine Soul Urge! He didn't get to see his friends next door on that visit!

"We've been together eighteen years now. It hasn't been easy at times, but when two people love each other the way we do, you make allowances. I believed what you said in your class, but now I know it's true!"

CHAPTER NINE

Color

*C*olors have always had symbolic associations. What color symbolizes the purity and innocence of a young bride better than white? Likewise, because green has a strong affinity with nature, it symbolizes growth and fertility. Thousands of years ago, people noticed the abundant growth of the plant kingdom and decided green was the perfect color to symbolize this. Primitive people had little interest in the beauty or nature of different colors, but were intensely aware of color symbolism.[59]

---

59.   Faber Birren, *Color Psychology and Color Therapy* (Secaucus: The Citadel Press, 1961), 3.

Red earth and yellow sun came to symbolize life, as primitive people could hunt during the daytime. The nighttime was dangerous, and black became associated with fear and death. Even today, black is considered a negative color, while white is almost always positive. People believed everything was created from the four elements and associated a color with each one: earth is green, air is yellow, fire is red, and water is blue. Creating color symbolism in this way enabled the people to give a personal, human shape to a dangerous and alien world.

The Mountain of God, built about 2,300 B.C.E., contained a four-story tower, known as a ziggurat. Each level was a different color that had symbolic meaning. These four levels represented the underworld, the earth, heaven, and the sun.[60] The remains of several other ziggurats have been discovered. The Great Temple of Nebuchadnezzar at Barsippa was dedicated to the seven planets, and was decorated with the colors that symbolized each one:

Saturn–Black

Jupiter–Orange

Mars–Red

Sun–Yellow

Moon–White

Venus–Green

Mercury–Blue

Color symbolism has been present throughout history. Obvious examples can still be seen today in heraldry, religious vest-

---

60. C. Leonard Woolley, *Ur of the Chaldees* (New York, NY: Charles Scribner's Sons, 1930), 151.

ments, and the colors worn by different university faculties. Today, color symbolism is often used intentionally to create a certain effect or feeling.

In addition to this, color has many other associations. Different colors affect our moods in varying ways. Some colors stimulate us, while others cool us down. We choose to wear certain colors, but avoid others. Someone who always wears black, for instance, would be consciously or subconsciously sending out a message to the world that he or she is disciplined, independent, and stubborn.

Depending on your particular circumstances, any or all of the colors of the rainbow can be used as symbols of love and romance.

Red

In Hebrew tradition, the name "Adam" means "red" or, possibly, "red earth." Red was the color of Ra, the Egyptian sun god. The Romans related it to Mars, their god of war. Blood is red, and consequently, red often symbolizes the life force. Red is the most physical color, and symbolizes the active, masculine side of life. It relates to passion, desire, and sexual gratification. It also provides vitality, energy, enthusiasm, and a lust for life. Every color has a negative side. The negative aspect of red is anger and rage. People who "see red" are experiencing the negative side of red.

Pink

Pink, a mixture of red and white, is the color most often associated with love. It can symbolize both universal and personal love. Pink is soft, gentle, nurturing, and caring. It has a warming effect that eliminates negative thoughts and feelings.

Orange

In the Orient, orange is considered the color of love and happiness. This is not surprising, as orange stimulates the sexual organs. Some paintings of the Garden of Eden depict an orange tree, rather than the more usual apple tree. Paintings of Jesus as a child sometimes have him holding an orange, too. This is because there is a tradition that claims the orange was the forbidden fruit of the Tree of Knowledge. Orange also works on the emotions and raises the spirits, creating feelings of positivity, confidence, and self-worth. It is interesting to note that the orange robes of Buddhist monks are intended to symbolize humility.

Yellow

Yellow symbolizes life and truth. It stimulates the brain, and enhances logic and clear thinking. When people fall deeply in love, the emotions overrule the intellect. It can be a good idea to include a small amount of yellow to ensure the mind is not completely forgotten. In China, yellow is considered a color of youth, innocence, virginity, marriage, and fertility.

Green

Green has always been associated with spring and new growth. This association extends to fertility, and the Green Man, the ancient pagan figure who represents the spirits of trees and plants. Green benefits the heart on both a physical and emotional level. It enables people to relax, and feel peaceful, calm, and well balanced. It's the color that people look for when they are suffering from stress or emotional upheaval. It provides sympathy and adaptability. It also, as you know, enhances love and fertility.

Nowadays, because of its association with nature, green is often a symbol of ecology.

Blue

Traditionally, the Virgin Mary wears a royal blue cloak. It symbolizes chastity, and a life of spiritual contemplation. Blue is soothing and cooling. Spending time by an ocean, lake, or river is calming and helps restore the soul. Blue was chosen for the United Nations flag because of its associations with truth, thought, cooperation, peace, and goodwill. As the sky is blue, this color came to be associated with honesty, truth, and the divine spirit.

Indigo

Indigo stimulates spirituality, creativity, and intuition.

Violet

Violet brings peace and tranquillity. It has always been associated with royalty and spirituality. This may have been because purple dye was extremely expensive, and only the very wealthy could afford it. Wrapping a baby in a violet cloth was believed to encourage a prosperous and successful life. Violet is a highly intuitive color that enables people to clairvoyantly discover and understand hidden truths.

White

White is a purifying color. It is positive in outlook, but also relates to spending time on your own. The custom of white bridal gowns originated in ancient Greece. The white marble temple of Athena symbolized virginity, and as a result, this color came to be the favorite choice of brides. Queen Victoria reintroduced white bridal gowns in the nineteenth century. White also symbolizes divine protection and spirituality.

Brown

Brown is a nurturing, caring, earthy color. It creates feelings of security and comfort, but can make it hard to express your emotions. It encourages worldly success, especially in down-to-earth, practical fields.

Black

Black is a sophisticated, mysterious, highly feminine color. It symbolizes the unknown and the unconscious mind. It is the color given to the planet Saturn. In ancient Egypt, it was the color of Isis. The black earth of the Nile also meant that black cats were considered sacred. There are still superstitions about black cats today. Black was also associated with the Roman God of Agriculture. His midwinter festival was renamed Christmas when it was adopted by the Christians.

Silver

Silver, the color of the moon, is feminine and sensitive. It balances and harmonizes other colors. It symbolizes purity and chastity.

Gold

God is associated with the sun. It is a powerful color that promotes positivity, wisdom, and understanding.

How to Send Love to the World

Pink is the color most often associated with love. This is a visualization exercise that uses this color to send love to the whole world. Some years ago, I was teaching this technique to a class.

One of the students said there was little point in doing it, as he felt that one person would not be able to make any difference to the world. I asked him to temporarily suspend his disbelief and to comment again after he had performed the exercise. Interestingly, his point of view was completely different afterwards. He found the exercise helpful in two ways. He felt that he had sent out love to the world. He also felt calmer and more at peace with himself and his circumstances and situation.

Sit down comfortably, close your eyes, and relax. Take several slow deep breaths, and focus on your breathing. Allow all the muscles of your body to relax.

Once you feel totally relaxed, visualize yourself sitting wherever you happen to be. People visualize in different ways. Some people can "see" clearly in their mind's eye. Others gain a faint impression, and others "see" nothing at all, but experience the scene in different ways. Visualize yourself in the scene in whatever way feels right for you.

Become familiar with the scene. Notice the furniture and furnishings, and become aware of any sounds, smells or feelings. Observe yourself again in your imagination. Focus on the area of your heart and feel the warmth and love inside it. Visualize yourself sending out love to the entire world. As you do this, imagine the area around your heart shimmering with a beautiful pink energy. Allow this pink energy to gradually expand until you are totally surrounded by it. It looks like a pink, cloud-like aura. Watch this pink energy grow and expand every time you exhale. Feel the sensation of sending your love to the world. Soon the pink energy fills the entire room you are in.

In your imagination, remain where you are, but keep sending out loving thoughts to the world. As you do this, allow the pink energy to expand to fill the building you are in, and then to gradually encompass a larger and larger area.

Change your perspective, so you are now a few hundred feet up in the air. Watch the pink energy gradually expand to fill the entire scene. Visualize your love continuing to grow and expend until it has encompassed the whole world.

Allow yourself to bathe in the gentle loving pink energy for as long as you wish. When you feel ready, take three slow deep breaths, open your eyes, stretch luxuriously, and then spend a minute or two thinking about what you have achieved before continuing with your day.

You will get up feeling invigorated, revitalized, and with loving feelings toward yourself and all humanity. These feelings will subtly change your approach to life, and you will find yourself more loving and compassionate in every situation you find yourself within.

Josephine's Experience

Josephine decided to use color symbolism after attending a feng shui class. She was fascinated to discover that red in the bedroom would spice up her love life. She and her husband, Paul, had been happily married for twenty-seven years, but their love life was virtually non-existent.

"It didn't happen overnight," she told me. "We had a great sex life initially. I'm not sure what happened, really. Maybe it was bringing up four children. Paul was busy at work and I was busy at home. When we got to bed, all we wanted to do was sleep. So, making love became less and less frequent.

"At the feng shui course, I decided to experiment and see what would happen. I didn't go berserk and replace the wallpaper in our bedroom. All I did was buy two red ornaments of people riding a horse. They're made of glass. One is a handsome man and the other a gorgeous woman. I thought having a pair, especially a man and a woman, would help.

"I had them in the dining room when Paul came home. I showed them to him, and said I thought they looked cute. I didn't say why I'd bought them. Paul was pretty non-committal about them, but he always is with ornaments. Our home would be purely functional if it was left to him.

"Anyway, after dinner, I put them on my dressing table. I saw Paul looking at them when we went to bed, but he didn't say anything. I was a bit excited that night, I must admit, but the ornaments did nothing for Paul. He hopped into bed and went straight to sleep.

"The same thing happened the next couple of nights. I was starting to think of the questions I should ask my feng shui teacher to make them work when, on Friday night, Paul cuddled me and then we had the best night of lovemaking I could remember.

"That started the ball rolling again. We're not like newlyweds, but at least we have a sex life again. It's better than before, too. I've told several friends about this, and the ones who followed my advice had similar results. We're taking a trip next month and I'm wondering if I should bring my two horses with us . . ."

CHAPTER TEN

The Tarot

The Tarot first appeared in Europe in the late fourteenth century. Its origins are unknown. At that time, few people could read or write, and pictures were used as educational tools. Most of these were religious paintings, such as the frescoes by Giotto. People meditated on these to gain insight and spiritual understanding. It is possible that the symbolic images of the Tarot were developed to help people reach new levels of consciousness. The symbolism of the Tarot was one of the main ways in which occult knowledge could be passed on when it was dangerous to talk about such things.

The Tarot is full of symbolism, much of it relating to love and romance. In fact, the Tarot could be considered a symbol system that leads to enlightenment. Many of the symbols can be interpreted using what we have already learned. The plants and animals in the various cards are examples. The numbers of the cards can also be interpreted using numerology. The color choices are also rich in symbolism.

The Tarot deck consists of seventy-eight cards, divided into two sections known as arcana. The word *arcana* is the Latin word for secrets. The Major Arcana consists of twenty-two cards. This has led many people to believe that the creators of the Tarot deck were familiar with the Kaballah, as the Hebrew alphabet contains twenty-two, highly symbolic letters. According to the Kabbalah, these twenty-two letters represent the entire universe. Twenty-two is also considered a Master Number in numerology. The cards of the Major Arcana could be called the paths to initiation. The Minor Arcana contains the remaining fifty-six cards, divided into four suits of cards: wands, cups, swords, and pentacles. These correspond to the suits of a normal deck of playing cards. Seventy-eight is the sum of the first twelve cards (1 + 2 + 3, etc.).

Major Arcana Cards that Relate to Love

The High Priestess

Feminine insight, intuition, mystery

The High Priestess card symbolizes the virgin or maiden. The archetype of the feminine is the triple-faced goddess: the virgin, mother, and hag. The High Priestess card symbolizes the first of these. The High Priestess sits between two columns, one black and one white. These symbolize night and day, summer and winter, and consciousness and unconsciousness. Each is of equal importance to the High Priestess who sits between them. The crown she wears symbolizes the three phases of the Moon—waxing, full, and waning. This allows the High Priestess to dream, and gain intuitive insights. The screen behind the high priestess contains pomegranates, a symbol of fertility. In this instance, the fertility is likely to be the birth of new ideas, rather than pregnancy.

The appearance of the High Priestess in a spread of cards indicates that you need to look inside yourself to find the answers to your questions. Often these answers are learned through setbacks or disappointments. Consequently, when the High Priestess card reveals a romantic relationship, it is unlikely to be a happy one.

The Empress
Fecundity, motherhood, nurture, life force, creativity

The Empress symbolizes fulfillment. In most decks of cards, the Empress wears loose-fitting robes, symbolizing pregnancy. In the Universal Tarot, the empress wears green, which is the color of nature, life, renewal, and fertility. Beside her is a heart-shaped stone that has been engraved with the astrological glyph for Venus. The river and the forest behind her also show The Empress symbolizes fertility and fruitfulness. Water symbolizes life. The trees behind her are cypress trees, which were sacred to Venus. All of these symbolize the sensual aspects of the Empress.

The Empress can be related to Demeter, the Greek goddess of the fertility of the earth. She also looked after marriage and social order. Demeter was involved in ensuring the fertility of both people and the earth.

The appearance of the Empress in a spread is a positive sign, indicating fruitfulness, fertility, and expansion. It also symbolizes love, happiness, and sexual satisfaction.

The Emperor
Virility, fatherhood, power, leadership

The Emperor symbolizes fatherhood, virility, worldly power, and male authority. He frequently carries a scepter, sword, or wand. These indicate sovereignty and leadership, but can also be considered a phallic symbol. In the Universal Tarot, the scepter resembles an ankh, which the ancient Egyptians considered a symbol of life. The armrests of the emperor's chair show two ram heads. Two more decorate the top of his throne. These are an obvious symbol of virility and procreation. The ram's heads also symbolize Aries, the first sign of the zodiac. Aries is governed by Mars, which relates to fiery energy, ambition, lust, and desire.

It is always a good sign to see the Emperor card in a spread, as it means you are on the road to success.

The Lovers
Union, marriage, passion, desire

The Lovers card usually relates to love and romance. It always means that something pleasant is about to occur. Traditionally, the Lovers card showed three people, a man with a woman on each side, indicating that a choice had to be made. This shows that hasty decisions must be avoided, as the consequences could be disastrous.

Arthur Edward Waite reduced the figures to two in his Tarot deck, and most modern decks have continued with this. The two main figures in the Lovers card symbolize Adam and Eve, the first couple. Behind Eve is the Tree of the Knowledge of Good and Evil, complete with serpent and fruit. The apples on this tree symbolize temptation and the ability to determine right and wrong. The tree behind Adam appears to be the burning bush. In the background, between the two lovers, is a mountain that symbolizes climaxes and the ultimate in happiness.

The archangel Raphael looks down on the two lovers. Raphael represents the Air element, and this is symbolized by clouds in the Universal Tarot.

Although the two lovers are usually considered to be Adam and Eve, there are other possibilities. One is that the three figures tell the legend of Hercules who had to choose between two women, one symbolizing Vice and the other Virtue.[61] Many older decks show the three people as a young man, his mother, and the woman he loves. It symbolizes the fact that he needs to leave the security of the family home to start a new life with his lover.

Temperance

Emotions, moderation, harmonious relationships

Temperance is one of the seven cardinal virtues. In medieval art, a woman pouring water from one container to another symbolized temperance. Sometimes a water pitcher and a burning torch were used. This showed the water quenching lust. In the Tarot, the Temperance card shows an archangel pouring water from one container to another. This is probably Archangel Michael as he wears a solar orb on his forehead. This symbolizes the element of Fire, which relates to Michael. Beside Michael are

---

61. J. E. Cirlot (translated by Jack Sage), *A Dictionary of Symbols* (London, UK: Routledge & Kegan Paul, 1962), 194.

lilies, originally a flower with erotic connotations. In the Christian tradition, the Easter lily is known as the passion flower.

In a card spread, the Temperance card indicates a happy, harmonious relationship as long as the two people involved are prepared to cooperate with each other. It also indicates a time to open up and discuss your true feelings.

The Star

Hope, guidance, renewal, dreams, desires

This is one of the most optimistic cards in the deck, as it suggests hope and promise for the future. The maiden depicted in the Star card is young and naked, signifying innocence and purity. She has been associated with Inana, the Sumerian goddess of love and fertility. She has also been associated with Binah, the sephiroth of higher reason in the Kabbalistic Tree of Life. The young maiden is pouring water. The water poured on the ground makes the earth fertile. With another pitcher, she pours water into a pool of water. This symbolizes abundance. The message is that the future is both fruitful and abundant.

The Moon

Subconscious, change, creativity, fertility

Ancient people observed the cycles of the moon and noticed the different effects it created in the natural world. They also noticed the female menstrual cycle took twenty-eight days, and as a result, considered the moon to be the Great Mother, responsible for fertility, pregnancy, and new life. This explains why the Moon has traditionally been associated with women.

At night we see things dimly, and the moon came to indicate the subconscious mind. Objects that look sinister or alarming at night cease to hold any fears in the daylight. Consequently, this card sometimes has negative overtones. It is also a card of creativity, as inspiration also comes from the subconscious mind.

The two towers symbolize a gateway protecting the path that leads to the mystical realms of the moon. This lunar path shows the way to intuition, insight, and feminine wisdom. The two dogs symbolize the fear and attraction of this mystical path. The crayfish possibly symbolizes the astrological sign of Cancer, which is ruled by the Moon. It is also possible that the crayfish, crawling out of the sea onto the land, symbolizes mankind's evolution.

The Sun

Joy, happiness, optimism, enthusiasm

The Sun card does not have a direct relationship with love and romance, but when it occurs in a spread, it is a sign of warmth, happiness, and optimism. The sun can be considered the source of all life. In the Universal Tarot, some of the sun's rays are straight, while others are wavy. This symbolizes the dual qualities of warmth and light. The naked boy on the horse symbolizes the start of a quest for spiritual growth. The red banner symbolizes energy and action.

This card is a highly positive one to receive when the question relates to love and romance.

The World

Wholeness, satisfaction, success, fulfillment

The World card indicates the end of a cycle of experience. The wreath surrounding the dancing figure in this card symbolizes the womb, and indicates that a whole new cycle of experience is about to begin. The wreath in the Universal Tarot deck is comprised of laurel leaves and red ribbons. The leaves symbolize success, and the red ribbon is a sign of achievement. Another intriguing possibility is that the wreath depicts a zero. The first Tarot key, The Fool, is zero. The World, Key twenty-one, is the final card of the major arcana. The zero in this final card could indicate that the end is the beginning, and the beginning is the end. The heads in each corner of this card are the four "living creatures" of Ezekiel: a man, an eagle, a bull, and a lion (Ezekiel 1:10). They symbolize the four elements, the four directions, the four seasons, and the world itself. The naked woman in the center of the card holds two wands that symbolize the positive and negative energies that make up the world. Some writers have hypothesized that the woman is a hermaphrodite, but in the Universal Tarot, she is gloriously feminine, and is possibly Eve, dancing in a young, new world where perfection was possible.

Color Symbolism in the Tarot

Tarot cards are brightly colored in most decks. The color symbolism from the previous chapter can be used to uncover hidden meanings. In addition, there are also other symbolic interpretations that are unique to the Tarot.

Pink, for example, symbolizes anything human or relating to humanity, such as people and buildings.

Blue relates to secrecy, emotions, and the feminine.

Conversely, red symbolizes the masculine qualities of strength, energy, and power.

Yellow symbolizes the intellect, and is also used to depict the Sun and the earth.

Angels

Angels appear four times in the Major Arcana: The Lovers, Temperance, Judgement, and The Devil. Authorities on the Tarot have failed to reach agreement about the identity of these angels. Some people think the angel in the Judgement card is Gabriel, while others claim he is Michael. My view is that it is Gabriel, as this angel is blowing a horn and summoning the dead to rise up from their coffins. I think Michael is the angel depicted in the Temperance card. However, no less an authority than Gareth Knight feels that this angel is Raphael. I feel Raphael is the angel shown in The Lovers card. These apparent contradictions sometimes confuse people. The best way to identify these archangels to your own satisfaction is to meditate on the cards and see what insights and revelations come to you.

Angels are sometimes considered symbols of the relationship God has with his creation. They are more usually considered symbols of spiritual order.

The four archangels also symbolize the four elements:

Raphael symbolizes the Air element.
Michael symbolizes the Fire element.
Gabriel symbolizes the Water element.
Uriel symbolizes the Earth element.

Plants

The Tarot deck uses a variety of floral symbols. The rose symbolizes life. In the Tarot, a red rose symbolizes passion, and a white one, purity. It is interesting that a five-petalled rose is on the banner held by Death in the card of the same name. This is because the white rose on the black banner of death symbolizes life. The lily is another flower that symbolizes purity. Roses and lilies are part of the pattern design on the clothes of the tonsured monks in The Hierophant card. Roses and white lilies can also be seen in the foreground of The Magician card. These symbolize the integrity of the magician. The white lilies reveal the purity of his soul, while the red roses symbolize divine love.

The laurel symbolizes success and victory. The first and last cards of the Major Arcana contain laurel. The Fool has a laurel branch in his cap, and a laurel wreath frames the dancing figure in The World.

The pomegranate, symbolizing fertility, is found in both The High Priestess and The Empress cards. The pomegranate is related to the Greek myth about Persephone. Hades, God of the Underworld, kidnapped the goddess Persephone to make her his bride. Persephone's mother, Demeter, was goddess of the earth's fertility. She immediately made the world barren until Zeus forced Hades to set her daughter free. Before leaving the Underworld, Persephone ate two pomegranate seeds. This meant that she had to spend part of every year in the Underworld as Hades' queen. The grain in the foreground of The Empress card symbolizes Demeter.

Animals

Serpents have had a negative image throughout history. It was a serpent who offered Eve an apple in the Garden of Eden (Genesis 3: 1–5). The fact that snakes move without legs, live in holes in the ground, and hatch out of eggs has been a source of endless fascination. The forked tongue of a snake reminded people of deceit, yet the snake is also considered knowledgeable. Jesus said: "Be ye therefore wise as serpents, and harmless as doves" (Matthew 10:16).

Snakes have always been a sexual symbol. Their sinuous movements appear feminine, but their shape is phallic and also reminiscent of the umbilical cord. They also have an engulfing stomach, which can be symbolically connected to pregnancy.

Anita's Experience

I first met Anita when we were both teenagers. Almost forty years later, our paths crossed again when we both attended the opening of an exhibition of Tarot cards at my local library. Afterwards, I invited her for a coffee.

"You're probably wondering why I came to an exhibition of Tarot cards," she said.

"Not really," I replied. "The Tarot is extremely popular nowadays."

Anita nodded. "I used to have a boyfriend who was very interested in it," she said. "I think part of his appeal was his interest in things like that." She smiled. "That relationship finished years ago, but something he did with Tarot cards intrigued me."

"What was that?"

"Well, he never read the cards for other people. But every day, he'd put one Tarot card in his pocket. Whenever he had a spare moment, he'd pull it out and study it. He said that during the day, ideas would come to him about the card. He also thought the card placed him in situations which helped him understand its meaning."

"That's interesting," I said. "He didn't have favorite cards that he used regularly?"

Anita shook her head. "No, no. When Don was learning the Tarot, he took each of the cards in turn, to help him learn their meanings. Once he knew all that, he just took a card at random."

"Like a card for the day?"

Anita nodded. "You could say that. Well, anyway, after that relationship ended, I had a few boyfriends, and then nothing for ages. I remembered what Don said about the cards putting him in the right situation to learn what he needed to know about the card. So I chose The Lovers card. I put it in my purse, and looked at it whenever I had a spare moment. The idea was to use it so I'd end up in situations where I'd meet the right man."

"And did you?"

"Well, I met a few duds first. Maybe they were lessons I had to learn." Anita laughed and sipped her coffee. "But finally I met Jeff. He wasn't like the others. He was quiet, almost shy, but he has a great sense of humor. The strange thing was that he carried a Tarot deck around with him all the time. It's a miniature deck that his sister gave him. She told him it would bring him whatever his heart desired. He freaked out when I opened my purse and showed him The Lovers card!"

"Is the relationship still going?"

"Oh, yes. We've been together several years now. I still have the Tarot card in my purse, but now it symbolizes Jeff. We've both done courses on the Tarot, too. We figured that since it brought us together we had to learn everything we could about it."

On February 14th every year, millions of people around the world receive a Valentine's Day card. Everyone enjoys receiving one of these cards from a known or unknown admirer. This enjoyable custom is a successful example of how the early church managed to Christianize earlier pagan practices.

Long before Christianity began, people considered February a time of love. Spring was imminent, and birds were courting and mating. New life was emerging everywhere. According to English folklore, birds chose their partners on

February 14th. Geoffrey Chaucer, William Shakespeare, and Robert Herrick all referred to this ancient belief in their writings. Dame Elizabeth Brews also referred to this in a letter she wrote in early 1477 to her future son-in-law: "And, cousin, Friday is St. Valentine's Day, when every bird chooses itself a mate."[62] Because of this, Valentine's Day was sometimes called the Birds' Wedding Day.

According to folklore, the first bird seen on Valentine's Day will indicate the maiden's future:

> *Blackbird*: her husband will be a clergyman
>
> *Bluebird*: she and her husband will live in poverty
>
> *Bunting*: her husband will be a sailor
>
> *Crossbill*: her husband will be argumentative
>
> *Goldfinch*: her husband will be rich
>
> *Robin*: her husband will be a sailor
>
> *Sparrow*: she and her husband will live in a cottage
>
> *Wrybill*: she will never marry
>
> *Yellowbird*: her husband will be reasonably wealthy
>
> A flock of doves indicates an exceptionally happy marriage and a comfortable life.

The Romans associated February 15th with the goddess Juno, queen of heaven, and also wife of the great god Jupiter. Juno was the goddess of war, but also had a special interest in women and marriage. The Feast of Lupercalia celebrated her. On February 15th, young girls wrote their names on pieces of

---

62. Richard Barber (editor), *The Pastors: A Family in the War of the Roses* (London, UK: The Folio Society, 1980), 194.

paper and placed them in a drum. This was a lottery of sorts, as the local boys each pulled out a slip and, for the following twelve months, became the partner of the girl whose name they had selected. It was a day that celebrated life, love, and sexual pleasure.

The early Christians found it impossible to eliminate this eight-hundred-year-old tradition. They used lateral thinking. The Feast of Lupercalia was celebrated on February 15th, and St. Valentine had been martyred just one day earlier, on the 14th. It was a simple matter to move the festival one day and turn it into a Christian celebration.

Valentine was a pagan priest in the third century C.E. He converted to Christianity and ultimately became a bishop. However, little is known about Valentine, and it is possible that he is a combination of at least two Christian martyrs, both with the same name.

There are two versions of what occurred next. I prefer the first version, but the second one is more likely. Apparently, Emperor Claudius made a momentous and highly unpopular decision. Because he felt that husbands made reluctant soldiers, he abolished the institution of marriage. Valentine was not happy with this decision and continued to marry young couples. As a result of this, he was arrested, imprisoned, and finally clubbed to death on February 14th, 269.

The second version has the same conclusion, but is not as dramatic. Apparently, Valentine helped Christians who were being persecuted for their faith. As a result of this, he was arrested and ultimately murdered. In both versions of the story, Valentine is credited with restoring the sight of his jailer's blind daughter. On the night before he was killed, he sent her a message signed: "From your Valentine."

The Christians tried to eliminate the pagan and sexual connotations of February 14th by associating it with the little known St. Valentine. However, the popular lottery continued, much to the distress of the clergy. In 496 C.E., Pope Galasius tried to resolve this by substituting the names of Christian saints for the young girls. The boys had to emulate as much as possible the life of the saint they had selected. Somehow, this failed to capture people's imaginations and soon the names of young girls were being used again.

As time went on, people became less satisfied at choosing a partner by chance. They wanted to choose for themselves. Consequently, on February 14th, they sent a gift or message to the person they were most attracted to. Often, these messages were sent anonymously, putting the girl in the difficult position of having to identify the sender.

The oldest known Valentine's message in existence dates back to 1415 and can be seen in the British Museum. Charles, Duke of Orleans, wrote it to his wife, while he was imprisoned in the Tower of London.

The custom grew over the years. Samuel Pepys recorded several Valentine's Days in his diary. On February 14th, 1661, he indicates that Valentine's greetings can be given to friends: "So up I went and took Mrs. Martha for my Valentine (which I do only for complacency), and Sir W. Batten, he go[es] in the same manner to my wife. And so we were very merry." On

February 14th, 1667, he wrote: "This morning came up to my wife's bedside, I being up dressing myself, little Will Mercer to be her Valentine; and brought her name writ upon blue paper in gold letters, done by himself, very pretty—and we were both well pleased with it. But I am also this year my wife's Valentine, and it will cost me five pounds—but that I must have laid out if we had not been Valentines. So to bed."[63]

Valentine's Day cards were first exchanged in the sixteenth century. This means they are possibly the oldest of all greeting cards. In the eighteenth century, Valentine's greeting cards became part of the American tradition. They were usually handmade, and contained a verse and pen and ink drawings. Toward the end of this century, books and pamphlets were published to help people compose their Valentine's Day messages. Commercially produced cards, known as "mechanical valentines," were introduced and quickly became popular. In 1840, a talented artist and businesswoman, Esther Howland, began producing Valentine's Day cards in the United States. Most of her beautifully presented lace cards sold for between five and ten dollars, but a few sold for up to thirty-five dollars.

The nineteenth century Valentine's Day cards made great use of the secret language of flowers, which conveyed much more than the words could. In Charles Dickens' *Pickwick Papers,* Sam Weller advised his master: "Never sign a Valentine with your own name." Valentine's cards are usually sent anonymously, and it is still considered bad luck to sign one with your name.

---

63. Little Will Mercer was the son of Samuel Pepys's landlord, and the brother of his wife's companion, Mary Mercer.

Cards are not the only gifts that have been used on Valentine's Day. Traditionally, painted and decorated seashells were used as Valentine's Day gifts. [64]

From the seventeenth to nineteenth centuries, gloves and gauntlets were the most popular Valentine's Day gifts. This is because they symbolized honesty, integrity, and good intentions. Today the most popular gifts are chocolate and jewelry.

In 1902, a small candy company in New England began making heart-shaped candy with a brief message inscribed on it. Most of the original 125 messages, such as "Be Mine" and "Kiss Me," are still being used today. However, some phrases became outdated and have been replaced with more contemporary messages. [65]

The crocus marks the start of spring, and was believed to bloom on Valentine's Day. The crocus symbolizes the joys and pleasures of young love.

Valentine's Day has been banned on more than one occasion. However, the church was never able to entirely eliminate a day devoted to celebrating the joys of physical love.

Greg's Experience

Greg is a gourmet chef who is happiest when he is creating beautiful food. He owns a busy restaurant, which takes up most of his time. He is wealthy, charming, witty, and ruggedly handsome. It is hard to understand how he reached his middle forties without getting married.

---

64.   Peter Bently, *The Book of Love Symbols* (San Francisco, CA: Chronicle Books, 1995), 21.

65.   Denny Lee and Josh Stoneman, *Symbols of Love* (New York, NY: Assouline Publishing, Inc., 2002), 32.

"It's a combination of things," he told me, late one evening, when we were sharing a bottle of wine. "I spent years building up my restaurant, so you could say I was out of circulation for a long time. I had a few girlfriends at school. Not many, 'cause I used to be very shy. I had one serious girlfriend in my early twenties, but she found someone else while she was away at college. I had another several years later, and I thought that was going to last. But she got fed up with the amount of time I spent working. After that, I just focused on my career."

"Didn't you want to settle down?"

Greg shrugged his shoulders. "Of course, but it was priorities. It took years of hard work to get established. Only after that did I really start thinking about long-term relationships."

"You're in one now. How did that happen?"

Greg laughed. "I'm not s'posed to tell anyone about this. Debbie was one of my regular customers. I knew she didn't have a partner as she always came with two or three girlfriends. I'd hear them moaning about the lack of men in their lives. Over time, I got to know Debbie well enough to exchange jokes, and she told me a bit about her life, and I told her about mine. So I knew where she worked. Valentine's Day was coming up. I didn't want to send a card, as I wanted her to know who'd sent it. So I made her a special cake, and had someone deliver it to her at work. That night she came in on her own. We were busy, being Valentine's Day. She had a special look in her eyes and a big smile on her face. She sat at the bar for forty-five minutes before we could get her a table. I took her through to the restaurant, sat her down, and then sat opposite her. For the first time in seven years, I had my staff wait on me. It was an amazing evening. My staff insisted that I escort her home. I stayed the night, and, well, I guess I've stayed there almost every night since."

"All thanks to your Valentine's Day cake?"

Greg grinned. "That's right. I'm very grateful to that cake. Without it, I'd probably still be feeling lonely and miserable."

There is a strong connection between food and love. Both can be extremely sensual experiences. John Keats (1795–1820), the English poet, used the metaphor of food to describe Porphyro and Madeline's lovemaking in his famous poem, "The Eve of St. Agnes." Strong feelings of love and desire are often described in terms of physical appetite, which may or may not be fulfilled. Preparing food for a loved one has significant romantic associations, while sharing food can be an intimate and arousing experience.

Certain foods, known as aphrodisiacs, are believed to enhance the sexual appetite. Garlic, oysters, and truffles are the best known. However, the oldest aphrodisiac of all must be the forbidden fruit in the Garden of Eden. The Bible explains what happened to Adam and Eve after they had eaten it: "And the eyes of them both were opened, and they knew that they were naked" (Genesis 3:7). John Milton described this scene in much greater detail in *Paradise Lost*:

> *But that false fruit*
> *Far other operation first displayed,*
> *Carnal desire inflaming. He on Eve*
> *Began to cast lascivious eyes; she him*
> *As want only repaid; in lust they burn.*

The ancient Greeks and Romans knew their gods consumed ambrosia and nectar, the food and drink of the gods. This not only kept them forever young, but also enabled them to enjoy constant sexual activity.

Asparagus

Asparagus was recommended as an aphrodisiac in *The Perfumed Garden* by Shaik al-Nefwazi, a famous sixteenth century Arabian book on sexual lore. Nicholas Culpeper (1616–1654), the English astrologer and herbalist, wrote: "(asparagus) stirreth up bodily lust in man and woman."

Beans

St. Jerome banned beans from nunneries, as he thought they would inflame the passions of the nuns. Pythagoras would not allow his followers to eat beans either, for the same reason.

Broad beans were considered an aphrodisiac in Italy, but they had to be young and fresh.

Celery

During the Middle Ages, celery was used as a charm to produce boy babies. The celery had to be secretly placed under the bed of a pregnant woman. If the first name she spoke after this had been done was that of a man, she would produce a boy.

In the eighteenth century, celery soup was believed to have aphrodisiacal qualities.

Champagne

Any wine, in moderation, can have an aphrodisiacal effect. However, the drink that symbolizes love and romance more than any other is champagne. Everything about it, from the pop of the cork to the bursting of the bubbles in the mouth, is romantic, making this the drink of choice for any special occasion. Champagne also has an immediate effect, as the bubbles allow the alcohol to enter the bloodstream easily.

Chocolate

Chocolate has been considered a symbol of love and romance for hundreds of years. Chocolate contains phenylethylamine, an endorphin that provides energy and creates feelings of joy, happiness, and euphoria. As levels of phenylethylamine in the brain increase when people fall in love, it is not surprising thatpeople enjoy consuming chocolate to briefly recapture these feelings.

About three thousand years ago, the Olmec people lived on the Gulf of Mexico. As their language included the word "cacao," it appears that they were the first people to cultivate the cacao tree and consume chocolate.[66]

When Hernán Cortés (1485–1547) and his men landed in Mexico in 1519, they found the Emperor Montezuma II and his subjects drinking xocolatyl, a mixture of seeds from the cacao tree, pepper, and corn. The Aztecs considered chocolate to be both a spiritual aid and a powerful aphrodisiac. Although the emperor always drank xocolatyl before visiting his harem, it was far too bitter for Cortés and his men. Nuns discovered it made a pleasant and invigorating drink when mixed with vanilla and sugar. However, it wasn't long before the clergy were advised not to partake of it. In *The Food of the Gods*, Brandon Head wrote: "(chocolate was) a violent inflamer of passions, which should be prohibited to the monks."[67]

Despite protests from people who thought chocolate would mark the end of civilization, chocolate houses became popular all over Europe in the seventeenth century. Princess María Theresa, who married King Louis XIII in 1660, said: "Chocolate and the King are my only passions."[68] I find it fascinating that she placed chocolate before her husband.

Figs

The fig has always been considered a sensual fruit. In China, it was given to young lovers to symbolize the pleasures of love. The Greeks dedicated it to love and believed it increased fertil-

---

66. Christine France, *The Chocolate Cookbook* (London, UK: Lorenz Books, 2002), 8.

67. Brandon Head, *The Food of the Gods* (London, UK: R. Brimley Johnson, 1903), 28.

68. Princess María Theresa, quoted in *The Chocolate Cookbook* by Christine France, 13.

ity. Figs contain potassium, which explains why the fig has an aphrodisiacal effect.

Garlic

Garlic, like onions, is an effective aphrodisiac only when both people consume it. Garlic has numerous health benefits, including purifying the blood and increasing stamina and energy. These benefits may have helped garlic achieve such a high reputation as an aphrodisiac.

Honey

The ancient Egyptians used honey as a remedy for a variety of different ailments. They also used it as a source of instant energy. Sweetmeats made from honey were popular in Arabia, as they provided lovers with additional energy. Honey also reverses some of the effects of alcohol, making a honey-based sweet the perfect dessert after a romantic dinner.

Onions

The ancient Romans thought the entire onion family possessed aphrodisiacal qualities. Martial (c. 40 C.E.–104), the Roman poet, is best known for his twelve books of epigrams, which include: "If your wife is old and your member exhausted, resort to the humble onion."

Oysters

In Greek mythology, Aphrodite, the goddess of love, came from the sea on an oyster shell. No wonder the oyster has always been considered an aphrodisiac. In fact, Roman emperors thought oysters were so effective in this regard that they were prepared to pay for them by their weight in gold. According to his *Memoirs*, Giacomo Casanova (1725–1798), the famous adventurer whose name is synonymous with seduction, consumed fifty raw oysters every morning. He did this while enjoying a bath with the lady he had seduced the previous evening. Oysters contain zinc, an element that increases testosterone production.

Potatoes

It is hard to believe today that the humble potato was once a symbol of love, and consumed for its apparent aphrodisiacal effects. In the sixteenth century, people believed that potatoes would restore the virility of older men. William Shakespeare alluded to this belief in *The Merry Wives of Windsor* when he had Sir John Falstaff say: "Let the sky rain potatoes" (Act V, Scene V). As potatoes became more readily available, this belief disappeared.

Strawberries

Strawberries have always symbolized eroticism and sexual pleasure. This may be because they look like nipples, but is more likely to be because of their juicy sweetness and texture.

Truffles

The truffle is a fungus that grows on the roots of trees. The ancient Romans were extremely fond of it, because of its aphrodisiacal qualities. Giacomo Casanova used truffles as an aphrodisiac. King Louis XIV of France was reputed to eat a pound of truffles a day. Napoleon Bonaparte also remained virile with a regular supply of truffles. Jean Anthelme Brillat-Savarin (1755–1826), the French politician, author, and arguably world's greatest gastronome, interviewed many people while researching the aphrodisiacal effects of the truffle. He discovered that the truffle awakened "erotic and gastronomic ideas both in the sex wearing petticoats and in the bearded portion of humanity."[69] M. Brillat-Savarin devoted six pages to truffles in his book, *La Physiologie du gout*,[70] which is full of delightful anecdotes, including one about a hostess who narrowly escaped being ravished after serving a hen stuffed with truffles to a male guest.

Vodka

Alcohol is a form of anaesthetic that dulls the higher nervous centers removing inhibitions, good judgment, and fears of any consequences in the process. It is not a stimulant, and certainly does nothing to enhance sexual performance. As a result, although alcohol is frequently associated with love and romance, few alcoholic beverages can claim to symbolize these things. Vodka is one of them.

Vodka has become a sophisticated symbol of love because of its clear, pure taste. A toast of vodka between two people who care for each other can be a powerful symbol of their love and passion. However, it is still alcoholic, and moderation is required.

Gwen's Experience

As Gwen is a gourmet chef, I was not surprised to learn that she chose food as her way to restore her relationship. She was

---

69. Jean Anthelme Brillat-Savarin, quoted in *The Charms of Love* by Edward S. Gifford (London, UK: Faber and Faber Limited, 1963), 180.

70. Jean Anthelme Brillat-Savarin, *La Physiologie du gout* (Paris: self-published, 1825). An English translation was published in 1960 as *The Physiology of Taste* by Anthelme Brillat-Savarin (London, UK: Constable and Company, Limited).

eighteen years old when she married Harry. They had been married for thirty years when I first met them. At that time they were, as Gwen put it, "Buddies, not lovers." "He's my best friend," she told me. "I love him dearly, and I know he loves me, but our love life is dismal. It's sad, because it used to be fantastic."

"Have you discussed it with Harry?" I asked.

Gwen shook her head. "He won't talk about it. The last few times we tried were failures, and I think he's worried about it. He always goes into himself when things aren't right."

"How about a romantic evening?" I suggested. "Good food, wine, candlelight, soft music, and anything else you can think of."

"No, no," Gwen said. "Harry would see right through that."

"Is there a special occasion coming up? You could use it as an excuse for a celebration."

Gwen shook her head. Then she paused for a few seconds, gazing upwards. A look of mischief crossed her face, and she laughed. "You know, we've no celebrations for a while, but you've given me an idea. I'll let you know how we get on."

As Gwen and Harry were obviously still in love, I did not worry about them. However, I was delighted to hear from Gwen a couple of months later.

"How are you getting on?" I asked.

"Wonderful, thank you," Gwen replied. "I started thinking about foods that supposedly spiced up your love life. Oysters and things like that. Then I thought of something even better. I started cooking Harry all his favorite foods. No candlelight, no music, and just a bit of wine. He started becoming a bit more affectionate after the first meal. However, it took a week before there was any action. That was good for both of us. Then nothing for another week or so. It took time, but now we're enjoying a good love life. Thanks for your suggestion."

"It wasn't me," I said. "I suggested you add all the trimmings. You did none of that, but you've certainly proved the way to a man's heart is through his stomach."

"I've been thinking about that. I think all food is a symbol of love. First, I choose and buy the food. I bring it home and prepare it. Then I serve it. That's all done with love. We eat it together, and then we wash up. That's love, too, as we're spending quality time together. What do you think?"

CHAPTER THIRTEEN

Perfumes

*P*erfumes and scents have been used for at least six thousand years. The first scents were burned as incense offerings to the gods. In the Bible, the sons of Aaron the High Priest, made offerings of this sort. "And he shall bring it Aaron's sons the priests: and he shall take thereout his handful of the flour thereof, and of the oil thereof, with all the frankincense thereof; and the priest shall burn the memorial of it upon the altar, to be an offering made of fire, of a sweet savour unto the Lord" (Leviticus 2:2).

Fragrances of extremely high quality have been made since the time of the ancient Egyptians. When Howard Carter opened the Tomb of Tutankhamun in 1922, he was astonished to discover scents that were still vibrant after three thousand years.

Our sense of smell enables us to recapture long-distant memories, many of which are symbolic. My grandmother wore a highly distinctive perfume. Whenever I come across someone else wearing the same scent, I am suddenly eight or nine years old again, listening to my grandmother playing the piano. Scents make highly evocative symbols.

Even air can be considered symbolic. The Greek Stoic philosophers thought air symbolized the soul. The pure, cold air found at the top of a mountain symbolizes "heroic and solitary thought."[71] Air laden with strong scent symbolizes the emotions.

Wind, air, and breath are closely related in symbology. The second verse of Genesis says: "And the Spirit of God moved upon the face of the waters." In other words, the Spirit of God moved like a wind or breath. Winds are commonly considered to be the breath of God.

Wind has a variety of symbolic meanings. It can symbolize instability and unreliability because it varies in degree and ferocity. Wind was considered a sexual symbol in China because it was an essential factor in pollination.

Air is one of the four elements of Fire, Earth, Air and Water. Unlike the others, air is invisible and is considered spiritual. St.

---

71.   J. E. Cirlot, *A Dictionary of Symbols* (London: Routledge & Kegan Paul Limited, 1962), 252.

Martin (c. 316 C.E.–c. 400), the patron saint of France, called the element of air "a palpable symbol of invisible life."[72]

Breath is universally considered a symbol of life. The ancient Celts believed it possessed magical properties. They believed they could obtain wisdom from the element of air. Mogh Ruith, a mythical druid, used his breath on a number of occasions to defeat his enemies. An epic poem called "The Siege of Drom Damhghaire" tells how he breathed on all the warriors who surrounded him during the battle. His breath made them all look like him. They then proceeded to kill each other, while Mogh Ruith escaped. On another occasion, Mogh Ruith turned three druids into stone by breathing upon them.[73]

The sense of smell works on the limbic node of the brain. This is the oldest part of the human brain, and it deals with memory and emotional responses. The olfactory organ at the top of the nose captures any scents and passes it directly to the brain. The olfactory organ is amazingly sensitive, enabling us to subconsciously sense ("smell") other people's states of health, sensuality, and emotions. In fact, we are subconsciously using all of our senses, all the time, as part of our survival instinct.

There are many ways in which we can use pleasant smells to enhance our lives. Perfume has been used throughout history to attract and captivate others. Essential oils are another way to receive the benefits of scent. Aromatherapists use them

---

72. St. Martin, quoted in *The Penguin Dictionary of Symbols* by Jean Chevalier and Alain Gheerbrant, translated by John Buchanan-Brown, (London, UK: Penguin Books Limited, 1996), 10.

73. John Matthews, *Taliesin: The Last Celtic Shaman* (Rochester, VT: Inner Traditions, 1991), 44–46.

to help people with a variety of problems. Incense also provides pleasant odors.

One of the best ways to make the most of a particular scent is to relax in a scented bath of herbs or bath salts.[74]

You can also heat essential oils on an electric oil burner. These can be obtained anywhere essential oils are sold. They are usually pottery or ceramic. All you need do is place ten drops of the oil of your choice on the burner, and turn it on. The burner heats the oil, releasing the scent, and filling the room with a delicate aroma.

You may prefer to use a spray bottle. You will need fifty drops of essential oil and fifty drops of oil soluboliser. Dissolve this in three or four ounces of pure water. Shake well. You can spray this on yourself, or use it as an air freshener wherever you happen to be.

Essential oils can also be used for inhalation. Add ten drops to a bowl of hot water. Place a towel over your head and the bowl, and inhale the vapor for two or three minutes.

A few drops of an essential oil can be used to scent a tissue, flannel, or cotton ball. This can be placed close to a source of heat to release the scent. This works very well in a car.

Using an essential oil can enhance the pleasures of a massage. The benefits are obtained both by breathing in the scent, and directly through the skin. You will need to obtain good quality carrier oil. Use about fifty drops of essential oil to every three ounces of carrier oil.

---

74. Scott Cunningham includes several recipes for bath salts in his excellent book *The Complete Book of Incense, Oils and Brews* (St. Paul, MN: Llewellyn Publications, 1989). These include baths for celibacy, love, lust, and protection.

Another method is to use a scented dream pillow. These are small cushions filled with fragrant herbs or flower petals. Dream pillows are a traditional method of encouraging a peaceful sleep and pleasant dreams. Dream pillows can sometimes be bought at craft fairs and gift stores. However, they are easy to make. They consist of a small cotton pillow, six to eight inches square, and a slightly smaller inner pillow made of muslin or fine netting. Mix the herbs and flower petals in a bowl. Add two or three drops of an essential oil. Mix the herbs again, and then pour them into the inner pillow. Do not overfill the pillow. You want the contents to be able to move around freely. Close off the pillow and place it inside the larger pillow. Use your dream pillow until the herbs lose their fragrance. Dispose of the herbs and replace with a new mixture.

Scents can be used as powerful symbols of love and romance. Here are a number of scents that can help you in this area of your life.

Aniseed

The scent of aniseed promotes confidence and self-esteem. It also enhances cooperation, diplomacy, and all dealings with the opposite sex.

Camellia

The scent of camellia enhances love and romance, and also helps stimulate long-term relationships.

Carnation

The scent of carnation stimulates virility, while also providing confidence and courage.

Cascarilla

This unusual scent smells like cinnamon and cloves. It provides enthusiasm and energy, and also encourages love and romance.

Cedar Wood

Cedar wood provides feelings of health and well-being. It stimulates home and family life. It is especially good for long-term relationships. It also provides willpower, persistence, and courage.

Chamomile

Chamomile allows you to release anything that is not working for you. It can be used to end a relationship gently. Chamomile is freeing, and allows you to eliminate bad habits and preconceived ideas.

Cinnamon

Cinnamon allows you to relax and enjoy life, while releasing the passion inside. It is a useful scent to use when you feel emotionally empty. It also provides enthusiasm and energy.

Citronella

Citronella works on the emotional level. It enhances virility and stamina.

Coriander

Coriander is a highly positive scent for people seeking love. It provides stimulation, sensuousness, and voluptuousness.

Cyclamen

Cyclamen is a good scent for people wanting to become pregnant. It is believed to enhance the attractiveness of the opposite sex, and make the wearer feel desired.

Cypress

Cypress is believed to possess aphrodisiacal qualities. It stimulates the emotions, while providing stamina and energy. It also provides comfort, support, and protection.

Eucalyptus

Eucalyptus allows you to free yourself from restrictive situations. If you feel hemmed in and unable to be your true self inside a relationship, eucalyptus will provide you with the necessary strength, courage, and confidence to break free.

Hawthorn

Hawthorn stimulates feelings of well-being, and is a good scent for people who have ended one relationship and are starting to look ahead again.

Heather

Heather is a virile, sensual, stimulating scent that provides energy and a positive state of mind.

Jasmine

Jasmine is a highly stimulating scent that increases the charm and attractiveness of the wearer. It allows you to make the most of the present. It also encourages conjugal love.

Lavender

Lavender is a nurturing and comforting scent. It provides emotional protection. It enables you to step outside yourself and your concerns, and gain comfort and peace of mind.

Lilac

Lilac encourages pleasant dealings with the opposite sex. It enhances communication and makes people more outgoing.

Lily

The scent of the lily enhances all dealings with the opposite sex. It improves creativity and intuition. It also smooths troubled waters and provides a degree of luck.

Lily of the Valley

The scent of the lily of the valley provides feelings of abundance and well-being. It enhances all friendships and provides affection and love.

Magnolia

Magnolia stimulates a desire for sex in both men and women. It enhances all forms of physical activities.

Marjoram

Marjoram allows you to eliminate feelings of loneliness, anxiety, and insecurity. It is calming, reassuring, and positive. If you are currently on your own, marjoram will allow you to enjoy social encounters once again.

Musk

Musk is one of the best-known aphrodisiacal scents. It heightens all the senses, and creates a desire for sex and physical contact.

Nutmeg

Nutmeg provides enthusiasm, passion, and energy. It allows you to overcome challenges and obstacles, and start again, without disillusionment. It provides both emotional and physical energy.

Oregano

The scent of oregano provides virility, stamina, and energy. It is believed to heighten the sexual response of women.

Rose

The scent of rose is invigorating and restorative. It provides comfort and love. It is nurturing, supportive, and sensuous. It enhances all close relationships.

Sage

Sage encourages platonic love. It provides wisdom, peace of mind, and the ability to see things as they really are.

Wallflower

The scent of wallflowers increases people's ability to deal success-fully with the opposite sex. It promotes both creativity and love.

Wisteria

The gentle scent of Wisteria promotes feelings of tenderness and love. It encourages reconciliation, forgiveness, and peace of mind.

Lucinda's Experience

Some years ago, I attended a weekend aromatherapy work-shop and happened to sit next to a middle-aged woman named Lucinda. It was a good choice. Lucinda had a wonderful sense of humor and saw the bright side of everything. I was amazed when she told me about her life, as she had experienced much more than her share of tragedy. Despite this, she was the most positive person in the room. She had come to the workshop as she was interested in perfumes and thought aromatherapy would help her find a new partner.

The lady teaching the course did not think aromatherapy should be used in this way. Rather reluctantly, she listed several scents that she thought would help Lucinda achieve her goal.

I did not see Lucinda for several months after the workshop. When I did see her, she was sitting in a park reading a book. She was delighted to see me, and we exchanged our news.

"Are you still using aromatherapy to attract love?" I asked.

Lucinda laughed. "Of course. I've discovered rose is the right scent for me. It makes me feel good. I feel inspired when-ever I use it. I'm sure it's attracting love to me."

"Have you found the right man yet?"

Lucinda laughed again. "You're so nosey! No, not yet. It's brought several men into my life, but none of them have been right for me. I think I've been sending out the wrong signals. Now, when I use rose, I visualize exactly what I want. You wait and see—it'll work!"

I visited Lucinda on several occasions after that. She was continuing to meet people, but "Mr. Right" was proving elusive.

"Maybe you've set your expectations too high," I said.

Lucinda sighed. "Fancy you, of all people, saying that. No, I'm prepared for it to take time. I know it will be worth the wait."

In fact, it took almost two years in total for Lucinda to attract the person she wanted. She still uses rose all the time. She told me that it symbolizes love for her, and using it all the time ensured she would always be surrounded by love.

*M*agical symbols can be used in a variety of ways to achieve the results you desire. You can use them consciously and unconsciously. Once you start working with symbols on a regular basis, you will start noticing them everywhere. They will provide valuable insights that will enhance your life in many ways.

Dreams

Everybody dreams, usually for about two and a half hours every night. In fact, you'd become ill if you didn't dream. Dreams allow us to release emotional thoughts and feelings that could otherwise cause major problems.

People have always been fascinated by dreams and the insights they provide. The Bible includes many examples of dreams and their interpretations. Joseph, the son of Jacob, provided several good examples. He was skilled at dream interpretation and correctly interpreted the Pharaoh's feast and famine dream, for instance. In the Book of Job, there is an account of how God used dreams to impart information: "For God speaketh once, yea twice, yet man perceiveth it not. In a dream, in a vision of the night, when deep sleep falleth upon men, in slumberings upon their bed; then He openeth the ears of men, and sealeth their instruction" (Job 33:14–16). Other ancient religious writings also contain numerous references to dreams and their importance. These include the Bhagavad-Gita, the Upanishads, the I Ching, the Koran, The Book of the Dead, the Torah, and the Tripitakas.

Almost 2,500 years ago, Chuang Chou, the Chinese philosopher, described the mystery of dreams perfectly when he told how he dreamt that he was a butterfly. When he woke, he wondered if he was actually a figment of the butterfly's dream.

Artemidorus Daldianus, the second-century Greek seer, wrote *Oneirocritica (The Five Books of Dream Interpretation)*, a hugely influential book that remained the main source of information on dreams until Sigmund Freud began studying them in the late nineteenth century. Naturally, people explored their dreams to gain insights into what was going on in their lives. Love, and all its ramifications, was obviously an important subject.

Many writers have explored their dreams. William Shakespeare used dreams for dramatic effect in his plays. Not surprisingly, dreams are a regular topic for poets. In his poem, "The Indian Serenade," Percy Bysshe Shelley (1792–1822), mentioned a romantic dream he had experienced:

> *I arise from dreams of thee*
> *In the first sweet sleep of night,*
> *When the winds are breathing low,*
> *And the stars are shining bright.*

It is interesting to speculate that Shelley was so in love that he thought about his love while awake, and then dreamed of her while asleep. Finally, he wrote about the incident in a poem.

John Aubrey (1626–1697), the English antiquary and folklorist, wrote: "The last summer, on the eve of St. John the Baptist, 1694, I accidentally was walking in the pasture behind Montague house, it was 12 o'clock. I saw there about two or three and twenty young women, most of them well habited, on their knees very busy, as if they had been weeding. I could not presently learn what the matter was; at last a young man told me that they were looking for a coal under the root of a plantain, to put under their head that night, and they should dream who would be their husbands: It was to be sought for that day and hour."[75]

Our dreams are full of images and symbols. Most people don't understand what they mean and dismiss them as strange dreams. Fortunately, it is not necessary to understand, or even

---

75.   John Aubrey, *Miscellanies Upon Various Subjects*. (Originally published 1696. Many editions available.)

remember, your dreams in order to gain help and benefit from them. While you are asleep, your subconscious mind works on problems and concerns that are important to you, and attempts to resolve them. This is why you can sometimes go to bed with an apparently unsolvable problem, and wake up the following morning with the answer in your mind.

However, you can gain much more benefit, and many more insights, by paying attention to your dreams. In fact, you will find so much information that it will seem absurd to ignore it. Your dreams will be full of symbols. Once you know what these symbols mean, you can interpret them to help understand what is going on in your subconscious mind.

The first, and most crucial, step is to remember your dreams. As you know, dreams quickly fade from our minds. I find it helpful to keep a dream diary on my side of the bed. A pad of paper or an exercise book is all that is required. When I wake up, I lie quietly for a few minutes and recall as much of the dream as I can. Immediately after doing that, I write down my memories of the dream using as much detail as possible. I find that while doing this, more and more information comes back to my conscious mind. I do not try to interpret the dream while doing this. I can do that when I have spare time later on in the day. All I'm interested in at first is to write down the dream in as much detail as possible. I also record how I feel upon waking. If I wake up feeling anxious, for instance, it is important to record that, as these feelings will have been created by the dream.

Sometimes I wake up knowing I've just had a dream, but it has already disappeared from my mind. When this occurs, I remain lying in the position I was sleeping in, and wait to see if any memories come back. I try to think of the first memory I had upon waking, as this usually leads me back to the dream. Most of the time this works, but sometimes it doesn't. I don't worry if I can't recall a dream. If it is important for me to know about it, I will either experience the same dream again, or the symbols will come to me in another dream.

The best time to explore your dreams is when you are able to wake up naturally. For most people, this is likely to be on the weekend. Before going to sleep, tell yourself that you want to remember your dreams when you wake up in the morning.

If you desire a specific type of dream, you should tell yourself that, too. You might, for instance, ask for a dream that will give you information about when and where you will find a new partner. You might request a dream that provides insights into the future of a particular relationship. You might even ask for a dream that explains why you have problems in this area of your life. Repetition helps. Whenever I request a specific type of dream, I mentally ask for it three times while I am drifting off into sleep. If I do not recall a dream that addresses the issue that night, I repeat the request the following night, and every night after that, until I experience the dream I require.

When you wake up, lie still for a few minutes. You may find that you can briefly return to your dream. Keep your eyes closed while you recapture your dream. Once it is clear in your mind, open your eyes and record your memories of it.

I prefer to write them down. You may prefer to record your memories on tape. Some people prefer to make a drawing of their dream, rather than write it down. All methods work well, and you should record your dreams in the way that seems best for you.

Once you have recorded everything you can remember, you can either evaluate the dream immediately, or put it to one side until you have more time. You may find that the dream makes perfect sense to you as it is related to what is going on in your life. It might be a strange dream that makes no sense at all, until you start looking at the symbols that appeared in the dream. Even apparently straightforward dreams need to be looked at closely. As dreams speak to us in symbolic language, the literal meaning of the dream may not be what it is really about.

You may discover that certain symbols appear regularly in your dreams. Obviously, you should pay extra attention to them as they have particular relevance and importance in your life.

Another advantage of keeping a dream diary is that you can review it whenever you wish. You may find that a certain symbol appears reasonably regularly, but not often enough for you to have consciously realized it.

Many years ago, I found that an ornate clock regularly appeared in a certain type of dream I was experiencing. I had not realized how often the clock appeared until I went back over my dream diary. These dreams almost always had me standing at a crossroads, unsure which direction to take. Sometimes I was dressed like the Fool in the Waite Tarot deck, while at other times, I was wearing my normal clothes. The symbolism of the clock was that time was moving on, and it was time for me to act.

A good way to explore the inner meanings of any symbols that appear in your dreams is a simple process. First of all, imagine that you are the symbol. Allow yourself to sense what it feels like to be this symbol. The final step is to experience actually being the symbol. You will be amazed at the ideas and insights that come to you when you do this exercise.

You may want to check out the meanings of the symbols that appear in your dreams in dream dictionaries. Remember that you are the best person to interpret your own dreams. The meaning you give to a specific symbol may not agree with what you read in books. However, it will be correct for you. There are as many ways to interpret the symbolism of dreams as there are people to dream them.

Some people find it hard to determine the symbolism in their dreams. A good solution to this is to draw a picture of your dream, based on what you have written down. Use colored pencils and quickly sketch the basic idea of the dream. You ability at drawing does not matter. You can use stick figures, if you wish. Color in the background, as well as the main elements. You can include any conversation in a bubble, like a cartoon, or write it underneath.

Once you have finished the drawing, give it a title, and then look at it dispassionately. The colors will tell you the "feel" of the dream. A happy dream will include many bright and cheerful colors, while sad or foreboding dreams will include a large amount of brown and black. Think about the setting of the dream, and the people who are involved. Think about the actions that occurred. Take particular note of anything that appears out of context. The ornate clock I saw in my dreams is an example. Write down anything that occurs to you. You will find the symbolism easier to determine, and interpret, from a picture.

Lucid Dreaming

Almost everyone experiences what is called a lucid dream every now and again. In a lucid dream, you realize you are dreaming while you are in it. You are actually "in" the dream, and "out" of it at the same time. In this state, you can usually direct it anywhere you want to go. You may want to continue with the dream you are experiencing and see where it leads. Alternatively, you might want to use the experience to explore something completely different.

Twenty-four hundred years ago, Aristotle wrote about lucid dreams in his book *On Dreams*. St. Augustine and St. Thomas Aquinas also briefly covered the subject. However, the first person to seriously study the subject was Marquis d'Hervey de Saint-Denis, a French professor of Chinese literature. His book *Dreams and How to Control Them* was published in 1867.[76] Frederik van Eeden, a Dutch researcher, coined the term "lucid dreaming" in a paper he presented to the British Society for Psychical Research in 1913. However, it was not until the 1960s, when Celia Green, a British parapsychologist,

---

76.   Marquis d'Hervey de Saint-Denis, *Les Rêves a les Moyens de les Diriger; Observations pratiques* (Paris, France: Libraire d'Amyst, 1867).

wrote her book *Lucid Dreams*[77] that scientists started taking lucid dreaming seriously.

Lucid dreaming usually occurs during the REM (rapid eye movement) stages of sleep. The first REM stage occurs about ninety minutes after falling asleep, and lasts for fifteen to twenty minutes. The REM stage reoccurs about every ninety minutes, although this speeds up as the night progresses. As the REM stage also lengthens as the night progresses, everyone experiences more REM sleep in the second half of the night.

Some people are able to experience a lucid dream by asking their subconscious minds for it before falling asleep. I find this works well sometimes, but doesn't necessarily guarantee that it will happen.

Another method is to set your alarm clock at one of the times when you are likely to be in the REM state. Turn the alarm off and return to sleep. Without putting any effort into it, as you drift back into sleep, see if you can guide yourself into a lucid dream.

The most reliable method, at least in my experience, is to tell yourself before falling asleep that when you see something specific in your dream, such as your hands, you will become consciously aware of it. Some people are successful with this on their first attempt. Most people need to practice for a week or two before experiencing their first lucid dream. Once you start taking an interest in your dreams, and recording them regularly, it is only a matter of time before you'll experience a lucid dream.

---

77.   Celia Green, *Lucid Dreams* (London, UK: Hamish Hamilton Limited, 1968).

Dreaming and the Tarot

This is an interesting exercise that frequently uncovers information that was overlooked or not noticed in the dream. After you have recorded your dream and analyzed it, write down three or four questions that you would like to have answered about the dream. A friend of mine always asks six questions, using who, what, where, when, how, and why as the first word of each question.

Shuffle a deck of tarot cards, and deal out three or four cards to provide you with insight into the first question. Deal out as many as necessary, one at a time, if you feel the first cards do not provide a complete answer. Record your findings in your dream diary. Repeat for each question.

I have used tarot cards for many years, and find the familiar images comforting and helpful. However, you can use any other divination system you are familiar with. The I Ching, Runes, and regular playing cards all work well.

Meditation

Meditation has been practiced for thousands of years. People derive health benefits by deliberately relaxing their bodies and minds and having a brief break from their busy, everyday lives. When you meditate, you quietly withdraw into yourself and can reflect on your life and the world from a calmer, deeper, gentler perspective.

You can meditate in any position that feels comfortable for you. I like to meditate on a recliner chair. I prefer this to meditating on a bed, because I am less likely to fall asleep during the meditation while on a recliner chair. However, I also frequently meditate in a comfortable upright chair. All that matters is that you are comfortable, and can relax in the position you choose.

You can meditate anywhere, at any time, but in practice, the more comfortable you are, the easier it is to meditate. Make sure the room is warm and you're wearing comfortable, loose-fitting clothes. You might like to bathe beforehand. Do not overeat or drink excess alcohol before a meditation, as this makes it hard to get into the required meditative state.

Once you are sitting or lying down comfortably, close your eyes and take several slow, deep breaths. Focus on each breath, breathing in to the count of three, holding it for the count of three, and exhaling to the count of three.

Focus your attention on one of your feet, and think of the fine muscles you have in your feet and toes. Allow these muscles to relax as you think about them. Once these muscles have relaxed, allow the pleasant relaxation to drift over your ankle and into your leg. Allow the calf muscles to relax. Gradually allow the feelings of relaxation to drift up to the top of your leg.

Repeat this with the other leg. Once both legs are relaxed, you can allow the relaxation to drift up through your abdomen and chest, down each arm, and then into your neck. Feel the relaxation drift from your neck to your face and, ultimately, to the top of your head.

Mentally scan your entire body to make sure you are totally relaxed. Focus on any areas that still hold tension and consciously allow them to relax.

Now that you are completely relaxed, you can use this state to achieve a variety of goals. You may enter this quiet, meditative state to enjoy a "mini-vacation" for a few min-utes. Doing this is extremely beneficial to your body, mind, and spirit. It is a useful practice to enter this state and think about the blessings in your life. In fact, you can use this time to think about anything. If you are meditating to attract love and romance, you can use this time to reflect upon what is happening in this area of your life.

Alternatively, you can think about a symbol that relates to love and romance. You will find that doing this will provide added insights into both the symbol and what is going on in your life. You may think you chose that particular symbol at random, but in fact, you will have subconsciously chosen the symbol because it relates to your present situation.

Once you have learned everything you need to know from the symbol, take three slow, deep breaths, open your eyes, stretch luxuriously, become aware of your surroundings, and, when you feel ready, carry on with your day.

It is possible that the symbol will not provide you with the positive response you desire. Depending on what is going on in your life, you may receive negative feelings, rather than positive ones.

Because it is important that you return to your everyday life feeling positive and optimistic about your life, you need to add something extra to the meditation before opening your eyes. All you need do is think of something that makes you happy. Experience whatever it is for a few moments, and allow feelings of warmth and pleasure to flow through your entire body. Smile and allow the feelings of well being to expand inside you for as long as possible. When these feelings start to fade, open your eyes.

Creative Daydreaming

Creative daydreaming is similar to meditation, but can be done anywhere, at any time. Instead of consciously relaxing your body first, all you need do is close your eyes and think of the symbol you have selected. See what comes to your mind. Use your imagination to add other elements to this mental picture. You might want to add another person, for instance. You might let your imagination choose a suitable background, which you can alter or change, if you wish. You might ask the symbol different questions, and see what responses come into your mind. Spend as long as you can in your daydream. When you feel ready, open your eyes.

With practice, you will be able to do this exercise with your eyes open, exactly as you do with regular daydreams. The advantage of this method is that it can be done anywhere, and need take only a few seconds. I personally prefer to meditate, but when I'm busy, or want a quick response, I'll use creative daydreaming.

Create a Symbol Dictionary

As you work more and more with symbols, pay careful attention to the ones that occur in your life most frequently. Notice the effects these particular symbols have on you, and write them down. A book that has been alphabetized, such as a personal phone book, is ideal. By doing this, you will gradually create a book consisting of your own personal interpretations of different symbols.

Recently, I had an interesting example of how people interpret symbols in different ways. My wife and I were at a formal dinner. We hadn't met any of the people at our table before. I noticed the lady opposite me was wearing a small silver rabbit on a chain around her neck, and asked her if it was a lucky charm.

"Yes," she replied. "Rabbits bring good luck."

The man sitting next to her commented that rabbits were an ancient fertility symbol, and she shouldn't wear it unless she wanted children. Someone else said rabbits symbolized magic and the occult. By this time, the whole table had become involved, and everyone had a different idea as to what a rabbit symbolized. This shows that it is your own personal interpretation of the symbol that is important. When I discussed this topic with a friend of mine who is a professional comedian, he said that a whoopee cushion was his symbol of love and romance!

Ritual

A ritual is a ceremony performed for a specific purpose. Rituals are often performed with a spiritual or magical goal in mind. However, anything that we do in a certain, specific way on a regular basis could be considered a ritual. If you get ready for bed in the exact same way every night, that could be considered your bedtime ritual.

Rituals can be performed to help you achieve your love and romance goals. All you need to do is collect some symbolic objects that are pleasing to you. Make an attractive display of them on a small table. You might prefer to use the symbols to mark the perimeter of an imaginary circle that you will work within.

Sit down inside this circle, take a few slow, deep breaths to relax your mind and body, and then gaze at the symbols you have selected. Think of your purpose in collecting them, and the goal you want the ritual to achieve. If you come from a religious tradition, you may want to start with a brief prayer. Alternatively, you might want to ask the forces of the universe to come to your aid.

If you are looking for a partner, for instance, you can use the ritual to ask the universe to help you find the right person. Make sure that your request is specific. Choose a suitable age group for the person you desire. Specify any other requirements you may have. There is no point in attracting someone completely unsuitable.

Look at the symbols you have selected, and see what impressions come into your mind as you gaze at them. You may like to speak to the symbols, one at a time. It is better to talk out loud, as you will then hear what you say, as you say it. However, if there are other people within earshot, you may prefer to speak to the symbols in your mind.

Enjoy spending time in your magic circle. Visualize how your life will be once you achieve your goal. Imagine different scenes, and see yourself and your partner, inside them.

Finally, give thanks to the universe, and walk out of the circle. Carry on with your day, happy that you have done something to attract to you whatever it is you desire.

Mandalas

Mandala is a Sanskrit word that means "circle." Mandalas are designs that are usually circular and are constructed around a central point. In Buddhism and Hinduism, mandalas are frequently used for spiritual and meditation purposes, but they can also be used to gain access to your subconscious mind.

Carl Jung (1875–1961), the famous Swiss psychologist, began drawing mandalas shortly after World War I, and is largely responsible for reintroducing them to the West. Drawing mandalas had an immediate calming effect upon his patients. In addition, Jung discovered his patients could make order out of their lives by drawing and studying mandalas.

You will find it helpful to draw mandalas on a regular basis, as they will provide you with insight into your inner mind. All you need are colored pencils and a sheet of paper.

Start by drawing a circle, and then create a picture, design, or simply shapes of color inside it, using as many, or as few, of the colored pencils as you wish. I prefer to put my mandalas aside for a while before interpreting them, but you can examine them immediately if you prefer. Your choice of colors will reveal your state of mind when you created the mandala. Look at the mandala as a whole, and then examine individual areas of it. You may find several symbols inside the mandala. These have particular relevance in your life at the time you drew the mandala.

Date each mandala and keep them. They become a permanent record of your feelings and state of mind at the time you created them. You will find it helpful to look back over them from time to time. Mandalas are even more revealing when a series of them are examined together.

Collecting Symbols

The Chinese have "silent affirmations." These are objects that cause them to think of something else whenever they see them. A fish is a common example. The average Westerner will pause and look at goldfish in a tank. He or she will find it relaxing to look at them. Someone from the Far East will have a different experience. He or she is likely to think of money and upward progress when looking at the same fish tank. This is because fish are silent affirmations that denote success. The origin of this dates back thousands of years when Chinese people observed fish leaping up waterfalls to get to the breeding grounds. This ultimately led them to associate fish with upward progress.

You know that a large number of symbols relate to love and romance. If you start thinking of love every time you see these symbols, they will become your own silent affirmations. This will happen automatically. All you need to do is place a number of symbols that relate to your goal in your home. Whenever you see them, no matter what you are thinking or doing at the time, your mind will immediately start thinking of love and romance.

You can use symbols to heal hurt and pain, also. One of my clients told me how she used a single symbol to remove a long-standing obstacle that was affecting every aspect of her life.

Beatrice's Experience

When Beatrice was ten years old, her cousin who was four years older sexually abused her. Although she had tried to forget the incident, and consciously distracted herself whenever it came to her mind, this incident had affected her relationships with every man who had come into her life.

When she was thirty-five, she decided to do something about it, once and for all. She bought a ceramic cat and placed it in her bedroom. She spoke to it every night before going to bed. Gradually, she felt better and better about herself. In some strange way, the cat was making her feel worthy of love once more.

A few weeks later, she visited a local pound and chose a black cat with a deformed ear. She chose this one deliberately, as he had been hurt also. She called him Thomas. He was timid, but gradually gained confidence as Beatrice looked after him and tended to his needs. In the process of doing this, Beatrice was able to tell her cat everything, and this provided healing for both of them.

Beatrice now has a partner. Thomas died of old age and has been replaced by another cat that Beatrice and her partner found at the pound. Beatrice says they did not choose her, and believes Tabitha chose them.

There is a law in the universe that says we attract to ourselves whatever we think about. If you spend more time thinking positive thoughts about love and romance, you will, in a sense, magnetize yourself and attract it to you. It may not happen overnight, but it will eventually.

Conclusion

*Y*our emotional well-being is determined by your ability to get along with, and love, others. Love is an essential requirement for emotional health. It is almost as important for physical health. When you love someone, and are loved in return, every aspect of your life improves. You recapture the joyousness and zest for life that is your birthright. You feel optimistic and confident that you can handle anything that life has in store for you.

More than one hundred years ago, Ralph Waldo Trine wrote: "Not to love is not to live, or it is to live a living death."[78] It is natural to seek love, but many people forget that they need to love before being loved.

Of course, love is never easy. Arguments and disagreements occur in even the happiest of marriages. Movies and television programs frequently present impossible representations of "true love." Many people feel unable to live up to these unrealistic expectations.

Some people expect to gain more from a love relationship than they are prepared to give. This is usually the case with love between a parent and child. The child receives more love than he or she is able to give in return. The parent's reward is watching the child grow up to become a happy, successful adult. However, this unbalanced situation is not a satisfactory basis for a long-term relationship between two adults.

I believe everyone has the capacity to love. However, human beings are complex organisms and love is sometimes restricted by beliefs, attitudes, and feelings that date back to early childhood. This could be described as emotional immaturity. People who are badly affected by these factors find it hard to love. They need to learn to deal with their anxieties and immaturity, and then balance this with their instinctive need to love.

Magical symbols of love and romance have been used for thousands of years to help people find and maintain the right relationship. I hope you will use the information in this book to achieve lasting happiness with the perfect partner for you.

---

78.   Ralph Waldo Trine, *In Tune With the Infinite* (London, UK: George Bell and Sons, 1899), 101.

Suggested Reading

Aïvanhov, Omraam Mikhaël. *Complete Works, Volume XIV: Love and Sexuality*, Part One. London: Prosveta Limited, 1976.

Allardice, Pamela. *Love Potions: Charms and Other Romantic Notions*. Chippendale, Australia: Pan Macmillan Publishers, 1991.

Becker, Udo. *The Continuum Encyclopedia of Symbols*. New York: Continuum Publishing Company, 1994.

Bellamy, H. S. *Moons, Myths and Man*. London: Faber & Faber Limited, 1936.

Bently, Peter. *The Book of Love Symbols*. San Francisco: Chronicle Books, 1995.

Birren, Faber. *Color Psychology and Color Therapy*. Secaucus, NJ: The Citadel Press, 1961.

Blakeley, John D. *The Mystical Tower of the Tarot*. London: Robinson & Watkins Books Limited, 1974.

Brillat-Savarin, Anthelme. *The Physiology of Taste*. London: Constable and Company, Limited, 1960.

Bryce, Derek. *Symbolism of the Celtic Cross*. York Beach, ME: Samuel Weiser, Inc., 1995.

Busenbark, Ernest. *Symbols, Sex, and the Stars: In Popular Beliefs*. New York: The Truth Seeker Company, Inc., 1949.

Chevalier, Jean, and Alain Gheerbrant. *The Penguin Dictionary of Symbols*. London: Penguin Books Limited, 1996.

Childre, Doc, and Howard Martin. *The Heartmath Solution*. San Francisco: HarperCollins, 1999.

Cirlot, J. E. *A Dictionary of Symbols*. London: Routledge and Kegan Paul, 1962.

Cunningham, Scott. *The Complete Book of Incense, Oils and Brews*. St. Paul, MN: Llewellyn Publications, 1989.

Cunningham, Scott. *Cunningham's Encyclopedia of Crystal, Gem and Metal Magic*. St. Paul, MN: Llewellyn Publications, 1988.

Dossey, Donald E. *Holiday Folklore, Phobias and Fun*. Los Angeles: Outcomes Unlimited Press, Inc., 1992.

Eberhard, Wolfram. *A Dictionary of Chinese Symbols*. London: Routledge and Kegan Paul, Limited, 1986.

Evans, Joan. *Magical Jewels of the Middle Ages and the Renaissance*. Oxford: Oxford University Press, 1922.

Fobes, Harriet Keith. *Mystic Gems*. Boston, MA: Richard G. Badger, 1924.

Fortune, Dion. *The Esoteric Philosophy of Love and Marriage*. London: The Aquarian Press, 1957.

France, Christine. *The Chocolate Cookbook*. London: Lorenz Books, 2002.

Gifford, Edward. *The Charms of Love*. London: Faber and Faber Limited, 1963.

Goldsmith, Elisabeth. *Ancient Pagan Symbols*. New York: G. P. Putnam's Sons, 1929.

Goodman, Frederick. *Magic Symbols*. London: Brian Trodd Publishing House Limited, 1989.

Goodwin, Matthew Oliver. *Numerology: The Complete Guide*, Volume 1. North Hollywood: Newcastle Publishing Company, Inc., 1991.

Green, Celia. *Lucid Dreams*. London: Hamish Hamilton Limited, 1968.

Harris, Bill. *The Good Luck Book*. Owings Mills, MD: Ottenheimer Publishers, 1996.

Heade, Brandon. *The Food of the Gods*. London: R. Brimley Johnson, 1903.

Hollingsworth, E. Buckner. *Flower Chronicles*. New Brunswick, NJ: Rutgers University Press, 1958.

Jung, C. G. (Translated by R. F. C. Hull) *The Collected Works. Volume Five: Symbols of Transformation*. London: Routledge & Kegan Paul, 1956.

Jung, C. G. (editor). *Man and His Symbols*. London: Aldus Books, 1964.

Jung, C. G. (Translated by R. F. C. Hull) *Mandala Symbolism*. Princeton, NJ: Princeton University Press, 1972.

King, Scott Alexander. *Animal Dreaming*. Warburton, Australia: Circle of Stones, 2003.

Kunz, George Frederick. *Rings for the Finger*. Philadelphia, PA: J. B. Lippincott Company, 1917.

Lee, Denny, and Josh Stoneman. *Symbols of Love*. New York: Assouline Publishing, Inc., 2002.

Liungman, Carl G. *Dictionary of Symbols*. New York: W. W. Norton and Company, Inc., 1991.

Mallon, Brenda. *Venus Dreaming: A Guide to Women's Dreams and Nightmares*. Dublin: Gill & Macmillan Ltd., 2001.

Matthews, John. *Taliesin: The Last Celtic Shaman*. Rochester, VT: Inner Traditions, 1991.

McCourt, Malachy. *The Claddagh Ring: Ireland's Cherished Symbol of Friendship, Loyalty, and Love*. Philadelphia: Running Press Book Publishers, 2003.

McCoy, Edain. *Celtic Myth and Magick*. St. Paul, MN: Llewellyn Publications, 1995.

Morgan, Harry T. *Chinese Symbols and Superstitions*. South Pasadena, CA: P. D. and Ione Perkins, 1942.

Ozaniec, Naomi. *Initiation into the Tarot*. London: Watkins Publishing, 2002.

Porter, Carole. *Knock on Wood and Other Superstitions*. New York: Sammis Books, 1983.

Shepherd, Rowena and Rupert. *1000 Symbols*. London: Thames and Hudson Limited, 2002.

Singer, André and Lynette. *Divine Magic: The World of the Supernatural*. London: Boxtree Limited, 1995.

Thomas, William, and Kate Pavitt. *The Book of Talismans, Amulets and Zodiacal Gems*. Whitefish, MT: Kessinger Publishing Company, 1997.

Tresidder, Jack. *Dictionary of Symbols*. San Francisco: Chronicle Books, 1998.

Tresidder, Megan. *The Language of Love*. London: Duncan Baird Publishers, 2004.

Trine, Ralph Waldo. *In Tune with the Infinite*. London: George Bell and Sons, 1899.

Webster, Richard. *Amulets and Talismans for Beginners*. St. Paul, MN: Llewellyn Publications, 2004.

Webster, Richard. *Feng Shui for Beginners*. St. Paul, MN: Llewellyn Publications, 1997.

Webster, Richard. *Soul Mates*. St. Paul, MN: Llewellyn Publications, 2001.

Webster, Richard. *Sun-Sign Success*. Auckland: Brookfield Press, 1982.

Weinstein, Michael. *The World of Jewel Stones*. London: Sir Isaac Pitman and Sons, Limited, 1959.

Woolley, C. Leonard. *Ur of the Chaldees*. New York: Charles Scribner's Sons, 1930.

Index